Endorsements

"This book is one of the most exciting works, on not just selling but connecting that I have read. Karol truly gives us the secret sauce to building and maintaining key relationships. This is so important because relationships are the foundation of successful agents and agencies. Building professional connections is one of the most valuable career skills for a professional to possess. A strong network of meaningful connections with others can help you find greater career opportunities while building meaningful relationships and excel all-round."

Ken Gallacher CLU, CLF, FSCP, LUTCF
Multiple Line General Agent
2011-2012 President GAMA International

"With *Positive Connectivity*, Garry Kinder and Karol Ladd set the new gold standard for excellence in life and business. Their hearts are authentic, the insights are fresh and timeless, and true servant-leadership undergirds it all. This book goes far beyond selling skills; it is a journey to deeper connections with others in life. Adding value to people's lives is a privilege and a stewardship; Garry and Karol's work here will guide you to make that investment."

Rick Loy
President, Consultants For Life

"Reading this book is simply astonishing on how you will encounter all of the needed precious info nuggets for more effective communication and assured self-development. Garry Kinder and Karol Ladd comment, coach, and better interpret for us the key components of working both with and through the people we daily interact. A must-read for one who values their interactions with family, colleagues, and clients."

Charles A. Calderwood CLU, ChFC
Calderwood Financial Strategies, Inc.

"While designed for sales professionals, *Positive Connectivity* is a powerful book that will have a lasting impact on anyone looking to put in the work to achieve growth in their personal and professional life. What a treat to have these two greats come together to provide this engaging, easy-to-follow read; providing us with encouragement, tips, stories, and a space for reflection. Thank you, Garry Kinder and Karol Ladd, for this wonderful resource and for your dedication and commitment to help improve the lives of others. Definitely not a one-time read... Let's all strive to be "Explorers"."

Kristan P. Lester, MS
E-Learning Program Manager
University of Nebraska Medical Center

"*Positive Connectivity* is an exceptional masterpiece released for a time such as this! It goes beyond delivering the fundamental principles that have been crucial since the early days of sales by serving as a poignant reminder in a time when these vital principles are frequently overlooked or forgotten. Within its pages, the book not only beautifully illuminates the art of building relationships but also acts as a guiding light for all types of relationships, whether they are personal or professional. It is a must-read that will empower and enrich your connections with others."

Mark Miletello, LUTCF, MLGA,
Co-Founder Insurance
Agent Trainers, Author

"Jack and Garry Kinder taught me and countless number of other professionals during the past 50-plus years, that the most powerful form of communication is that of the written word. This is evidenced by such documents as the Declaration of Independence, The Constitution of the United States of America, and The Holy Bible. Garry Kinder and Karol Ladd (Daughter of Garry Kinder) have come together to remind us of this, in this last Kinder Volume, *Positive Connectivity*. Through these written words we learn that relationships are built upon proven principles that will not only help us be successful in life but in business. By following these lessons, the best for all of us, is yet to be."

Ronald C. Price,
Senior Vice President Chief Marketing
Officer Career Life Agencies,
American National Insurance Company

"A match truly made in Heaven. The combination of Karol Ladd's practical practices of positivity and Garry Kinder's ever-green wisdom and experience make this a must-read for all salespeople. It is a road map to making lasting positive connections!"

                      Julie Davis-Colan, M.S.
                      Co-author, *Healthy Leadership:*
                      How to Thrive in the New World of Work

"I first met Garry in Akron, Ohio, when he was the General Agent for the Equitable of New York. He was an incredible field leader and made a huge impression on me as a young MDRT member. Years later I chose to become a General Agent and quickly realized I needed help, big help! I remembered Garry, knew he and Jack were consulting, and called him to teach me how to do my new role in a more professional and positive manner. He agreed and that began a journey of 41 years together as my mentor and friend. His book, "Building the Master Agency, The System is the Solution" is still the finest book ever written about being a leader in the life insurance-based financial services industry. I have consumed everything ever developed by the Kinders and believe that this final contribution from Garry and Karol is a must-read for anyone serious about excellence in their professional life."

                      Charles Parks President and
                      CEO of 21st Century Financial

"*Positive Connectivity* is not a book of theory, it is a book of experience and proven methods that every person in sales should read and refer to again and again. My good friends, Karol and Garry are right on the mark with this timeless information."

                      Honorable Ronald E Simmons,
                      Author of *Life Lessons from the*
                      Little Red Wagon
                      Founder and former Chairman
                      of Retirement Advisors of America

It's common knowledge that success comes as a result of a relentless execution of the basics. Yet the more successful we become, the further we get away from those basics which made us successful in the first place. P*ositive Connectivity* gets us right back to basics. I give you my personal assurance that if you follow the path laid out in this book, you will be successful.

Positive Connectivity is a working manual, a legacy and a tribute to the late and great Garry Kinder. The simplicity throughout the book is unmatched: How to make a positive first impression, how to communicate in a clear and concise fashion, how to develop the grit to succeed, how to know what your client is thinking and how to understand and define your purpose. All explained in a simplicity that borders on brilliance.

Like her dad, Garry, Karol Ladd has been blessed with a plethora of common sense. *Positive Connectivity* is only seven chapters long and every page is teeming with wisdom. Do yourself a favor. Read the book and apply the lessons for the rest of your career.

On a personal note, I knew Garry. Not the legend, but the man. He had more humble confidence than anyone I ever met. That humble confidence allowed Garry to influence the actions of thousands of sales people over the course of his career. He is missed.

        Donald A. Connelly
        Founder & CEO
        Don Connelly and Associates LLC

POSITIVE CONNECTIVITY

7 Essentials to Energizing Sales and Boosting Client Relations

GARRY KINDER AND KAROL LADD

POSITIVE
CONNECTIVITY

GARRY KINDER
AND KAROL LADD

Positive Connectivity:
7 Essentials to Energizing Sales and Boosting Client Relations

Copyright © 2023 by Karol Ladd

All rights reserved. No part of this publication may be reproduced, distributed, stored in a retrieval system, or transmitted in any form or by any means, including photocopying, recording, or other electronic or mechanical methods, without the prior written permission of the publisher, except in the case of brief quotations embodied in critical reviews and certain other noncommercial uses permitted by USA copyright law.

Published by Positive Life Principles, Inc
    Dallas, Texas

Title: Positive Connectivity
Author: Karol Ladd

Cover and Interior Design: Mary Foley

ISBN: 9798399951232

Printed in the United States of America

No patent liability is assumed with respect to the use of the information contained herein. Although every precaution has been taken in the preparation of this book, the publisher and author assume no responsibility for errors or omissions. Neither is any liability assumed for damages resulting from the use of the information contained herein.

For permissions, inquiries, or bulk sales, please contact:

Positive Life Principles
17110 Dallas Parkway, suite 280
Dallas, Texas 75248
214-695-2638
www.PositiveLifePrinciples.com

Dedication

*This book is dedicated in loving memory of
Karen Kinder Smith, who courageously lost her battle
with cancer in October of 2018. She was a loving
daughter to Garry, and dear sister to Karol and
a positive example to all who knew her.*

Content

Introduction: The Power of Connection. 1

Chapter One: Perception 5
    The Significance of What you Don't Say

Chapter Two: Presence. 16
    5 Secrets to Undistracted Conversations

Chapter Three: Power Words 27
    Dynamic Communication to Galvanize Sales

Chapter Four: Perspective 41
    Observing and Understanding How Your Client Thinks

Chapter Five: Potential. 53
    Boost and Fortify your Sales Expectations

Chapter Six: Preparation 66
    Peak Performance Doesn't Just Happen

Chapter Seven: Purpose 78
    Pursuing What Matters Most

Monthly Plan Template 97

Daily Plan Template 98

Final Note From Karol 99

Stay Connected 101

About the Authors 102

Introduction

The Power of Positive Connection

Our attitude toward others determines their attitude toward us.
EARL NIGHTINGALE

Greatness in sales is not a natural-born gift. It is earned by those who are willing to pay the price – those who are willing to learn, improve, and grow. The most effective people in the sales industry achieve their dreams through perseverance and a positive mindset. They recognize the value in building relationships with their clients and believing in their products. Channing Pollock put it this way, *"We should be content with what we have but never with what we are. The man who regards himself as a finished job is finished."*

Since you picked up this book, we assume you are not finished. You want to advance in your career, move forward in your sales and strengthen your connections with your clients. You know that you are not a finished product, but rather a work in progress. Our hope is that this book will energize you not only in business, but also in life. Generally speaking, success in both sales and in life is about the positive connections we have with the people we encounter. All things equal, people tend to buy from the people they like. All things *unequal*, people still tend to buy from the people they like.

In our technology-driven culture, making sincere connections with our clients is more important than ever before. We live in a society that is attached to our mobile devices. In fact, psychologists recently coined the term *nomophobic* (no-mobile phone phobia) for those who have a fear of being without their phones. Honestly, who doesn't have a bit of a sinking feeling when their phone is nowhere to be found? Perhaps we all are a little nomophobic now and then. Yet, despite the fact that we are constantly electronically connected, most people feel disconnected when it comes to human relationships. Whether we are engaging with friends, family, clients or business relationships, we must go beyond merely messaging or emailing to experience a true sense of understanding and connection.

One thing we have learned through the recent global pandemic is that people are not created to be completely isolated from one another. On the contrary, humans need authentic interaction. In fact, most people thrive through healthy connectedness – feeling heard, seen and valued by another person. In this book, we want to help you spark that kind of positive and lasting connection between you and your clients. We also want to encourage you as a person, to relate in a deeper and richer way with the people in your life, both family and friends. We recognize that people who know how to relate well with others make stronger and more successful salespeople. What are the key ingredients to help us initiate and deepen our relatability with others?

In *Positive Connectivity* we will introduce you to seven essentials you can easily build into your personal and professional life. Here's a brief look at the topics we will explore in the pages of this book:

Perception – Body language and tone of voice have a powerful influence on what you are trying to communicate to your clients. In a culture that tends to connect through texts and emails, a vast majority of your message may be missed or misunderstood. Recognizing the power of your non-verbal cues, we will examine the latest research to create confidence and increase your level of efficient communication whether in person or through technology.

Presence – In a distracted world, being present with the person in front of you is a vital key to developing and maintaining a loyal client base. Eye contact, mental alertness and focused interaction all play a key role in helping your client feel seen and heard whether you are meeting face-to-face or via video conferencing. In chapter two you will discover five crucial action points to ensure you stay on task, avoid distractions and remain attentive to your client's needs. Be present for every conversation.

Power Words – Although non-verbal communication speaks volumes, a well-chosen word is golden and can make the difference between closing a sale or losing one. You can either open up a conversation or shut it down simply through your words. In chapter three, you will examine power phrases that can help build connections with potential clients and impact current client relationships. You will also examine words and phrases to avoid. The right words at the right moment can be just the additional ingredient to improve sales as well as customer loyalty.

Perspective – People's backgrounds and personality types can cause them to purchase products from a variety of different motivations. When you take the time to consider your prospect's point of view, you develop a strong rapport and create better avenues of communication. Effective salespeople learn to listen and discover what the client wants. Chapter four explores innovative keys that open the door to understanding your client's buying personality and connecting with their specific needs.

Potential – No matter who you encounter on a daily basis, it is important to maintain a mindset of expectancy. Top salespeople anticipate a sale, rather than expecting a closed door. Seeing your client's buying potential makes a significant difference in results, and gives you a greater advantage in moving toward a solid sale. Instead of focusing on limitations, open your eyes to recognizing the possibilities and opportunities with each potential client.

Practice – Just as actors on a Broadway stage must practice their lines to stay on script, so great salespeople must practice their presentations in order to stay on target. Adlibs are for amateurs, but professionals are well-practiced. We want to help you build on the time-tested principle that great performance is always preceded by unspectacular practice.

Purpose – What is truly important to you in life and in business? As you consider your life purpose as well as your daily priorities, you become more effective both in work and in your personal life. Setting wise goals and reviewing them on a regular basis are the building blocks to staying on track and strengthening your sales. We will help you create wise habits and simple routines to allow you to live with less stress and greater accomplishments.

The Essence of Connections

The essentials in this book come from the many years of wisdom and practice in the field of sales by Jack and Garry Kinder, who have become icons and legends in the field of Life Insurance. In 1976 they started

Kinder Brothers International, mentoring and influencing the lives of myriad men and women around the world in the insurance business. Their personality, principles, procedures and philosophies are well-known in the industry and can effectively be applied to any area of sales. Kinder Brothers International has teamed up with bestselling inspirational author Karol Kinder Ladd to provide this powerful manual to help improve your sales performance and boost your productivity.

"About 70% of customers' buying decisions are based on positive human interactions with sales staff,' writes Lee and Julie Davis-Colan, co-founders of a Dallas-based consulting The L Group. We hope that you will find *Positive Connectivity* as an energizing tool that you can use to boost your sales, strengthen your connections and encourage long-lasting relationships. This book can also be used for group study to inspire your sales team, agency or entire company. At the end of each chapter you will find a section called "Recapping the Essentials." Here you will find a restatement of the essential truth presented in the chapter, as well as discussion questions and a positive action step to help you apply the important principles from the chapter.

Healthy and meaningful connections with others are usually preceded by your own emotional, mental, physical and spiritual well-being. Throughout this book we offer insights, inspiration and encouragement to help you experience a more balanced and meaningful life. A contented heart and mind can have a positive impact on results. Our ultimate goal is that these seven essentials will spur you on to develop and deepen the relationships in your life, whether with clients, family, friends or business associates.

Despite the number of transactions that are made online, there will always be a need for personal interaction and understanding when it comes to sales. Positive human connection is essential. In our ever-changing world of sales and technology, it is vital that we adapt our sales strategies and focus to maintain the human touch and positive connectivity for the 21st century.

CHAPTER 1

Perception

The Significance of What You Don't Say

Communication is a process (either verbal or nonverbal) of sharing information with another person in such a way that he or she understands what you are saying.

DR. H NORMAN WRIGHT

The old adage, "You can't judge a book by its cover," sounds noble; but the truth is we all tend to make judgment calls based on outward appearances. Typically, it only takes a few seconds to size someone up and create a first impression in a person's mind. Effective communication is not simply about what you say, rather it is more about what you don't say. Now, to be sure – your words matter, but that's not all that matters when it comes to getting your message across to others. Whether you are trying to build a positive connection with clients, customers or friends, your non-verbal communication should work for you and not against you.

From a firm handshake, to a confident smile, to the clothing you are wearing, you are giving a distinct message to others. Dr. Albert Mehrabian, author of *Silent Messages*, conducted several studies on nonverbal communication and found that only seven percent (7%) of any message is actually conveyed through words. He calculates that 38% is communicated through vocal elements such as voice tone and inflection, and 55% is communicated through nonverbal elements such as body language. According to Dr. Mehrabian's studies, 93% of communication is non-verbal.[1]

How do you begin to construct a cohesive connection with others without saying a word? With our techno-driven lifestyles, you may think that human first impressions are old school and not even relevant to discuss in a sales book – but technology is actually the reason we DO need to discuss the human connection and first impressions. The more entrenched we become in our online world, the more complacent we become to the reality of our visual and non-verbal cues.

There has never been a more important time for us to address the essentials of the person-to-person connection. We have become a generation of people who are comfortable behind the screen, but when it comes to actual human contact, the general population is progressively lacking confidence, professionalism and the ability to emotionally converse and connect. Let's examine several key areas of non-verbal communication that can build our relatability and open the door to potential sales.

The Power of Your Smile

It may seem simplistic, but a confident and sincere smile is an important part of the equation when it comes to communication. A smile speaks a thousand words. It says:

> "I'm glad to meet you."
> "You are important."
> "I care about you and am listening to you."
> "I believe in what I am presenting to you."
> "I feel confident about my product."

A smile welcomes others and makes them feel comfortable and relaxed. It speaks confidence, openness and understanding. Savvy salespeople know that a smile, even when they are talking on the phone, can be perceived by the listener and changes the tone of the conversation. Now you may be thinking, *but I don't feel like smiling*. We're not saying you should wear a fake smile – everyone can see through that. Be honest and real with how you feel, but think of a smile as a gift to other people – it's not about you. When we smile, the serotonin level (the happy hormone) in our brain is elevated. So, smiling can actually make us happier people! When you smile, you are not only building up others, you are also benefiting yourself as well.

When Kinder Brothers International co-founder Garry Kinder, was a young insurance agent in Bloomington, Illinois, his office was in the downtown square near the city courthouse. On days when Garry didn't have a lunch appointment, he chose to walk the city square, not only to get exercise and a little sunshine, but also to practice the art of smiling. He smiled at everyone he encountered and soon smiling became a natural habit. Interestingly, his daughter Karol learned the habit of smiling from her dad. While she was at Baylor University, many people knew her for her sunny disposition. In fact, that is one of the traits that attracted her husband, Curt, as he saw her delightful demeanor on campus each day. Give the gift of your smile to uplift others – you never know what doors it may open.

Essential Eye Contact

Your eyes are an endearing part of your smile, and they also play a vital role in strengthening the message you want to communicate to others. Eye contact demonstrates respect toward the people you encounter and shows them that you are interested in them.

Each of us can relate to times when we have been in conversations with another person and their eyes dart about the room. It's almost as if they are unconsciously saying, "I could care less about you and what you have to say. I am more interested in the other people who are here in this room." And let's be honest, we are all guilty of doing the same to others a time or two as well. The important thing is that we make a conscious decision from this day forward to stay connected in our conversations through eye contact.

Begin to build the skill of focusing, by concentrating on eye contact with every person you encounter, even if the only person you see is a co-worker, store clerk, or family member. As a positive side note, studies show that increasing eye contact with your spouse can surprisingly strengthen your marriage relationship. Eyes are the window of the soul, and reveals to people how interested you are in them. People know they can trust you when you engage with your eyes and are not afraid to look them squarely in the face. You will notice a vast improvement in your relationships with family, friends and clients as you let your eyes do more of the talking.

Of course, with anything in life, there is a healthy balance. If you stare continuously and too intensely, you may appear to be overdoing it or even a bit intimidating. Just relax, pay attention, and pleasantly maintain a normal amount of eye contact. Add in a nod or an expression now and then to let them know you are following along with them and understanding what they are saying. Maintaining eye contact speaks volumes without saying a word.

Positional Impact

Body language and position also demonstrate the level of interest we have in another person. A waitress who faces each customer as she takes their order communicates a listening ear, simply by the way she is standing. A teacher who turns toward her students and pays attention to them, gets her message across with greater impact than a teacher who sits behind her desk or hides behind a podium. A salesperson with a confident stance as she faces her client sends a message of reliability, knowledge and trust.

What does a confident stance look like? Here are a few suggestions. When meeting a client for the first time pay close attention to your position. Align your shoulders with the person's shoulders with whom you are talking. Push your sternum forward, bringing your shoulders back with a posture of confidence. Think about how it would feel if you were on the receiving end. Are you inviting others into your world or are you saying, "I could care less about you?" Or worse yet, "I don't believe in what I'm selling."

The way you carry yourself is an important expression of who you are. Consider the appearance of someone with poor self-esteem. Their shoulders are slumped, their head is down, and they typically will not maintain eye contact or smile. They are portraying the message, *I don't believe in my own worthiness, and you probably won't see me as worthy.* A positive stance, on the other hand, speaks a different message. It says, *I feel confident in what I have to offer you, and I know that my product will be the best thing for you.* A confident posture is not a prideful or cocky posture but simply portrays a position of strength. Sitting or standing tall, with shoulders back, head up, and hands resting comfortably, provides a positive impression and also sets your potential client at ease.

Let Your Hands Talk

Your hands do quite a bit of talking for you. A behavioral research lab, "The Science of People," recently conducted a study of TED Talk speakers, specifically examining their hand gestures. If you are not familiar with TED Talks, they are a popular series of short, powerful talks by a variety of people sharing innovative ideas. The online videos cover a multitude of topics from science to business to global issues. The research found that the most popular TED Talk speakers used significantly more hand motions and gestures than the least popular speakers. The Science of People claims that hand gestures increase the value of your message by 60%. That's a notable difference!²

Take a moment to consider what your hands are saying. Do they open communication or close it? Do they say, *I am nervous*, or *I am self-assured*? Are they inviting conversation, or do they imply that you think you know it all?

What are some of the best ways to use your hands? First, relax your hands and do what comes naturally and comfortably. Generally, when your palms are open (either on your desk or lap) this posture of your hands demonstrates truth, honesty, and sincerity. Some people find it calming and comfortable to put their fingertips together (like making the church steeple) and relax their hands on the desk or in their lap. Guard against fidgeting or touching your hands to your face. It goes without saying, no tapping your fingers on the table or playing with your keys, which shows signs of nervousness. Avoid hiding your hands in your pockets, as this tends to imply that you are uncomfortable or unsure of yourself. Besides, when you put your hands in your pockets, it encourages slouching and as we already talked about, you want to maintain good posture.

As we address the issue of hands, let's consider your initial handshake. You don't want to be that person with a limp handshake. You want your handshake to offer a positive picture of who you are. Generally, it is customary to stand when shaking someone's hand and offer a smile while maintaining eye contact. With your thumb extended upward and fingers pressed together, slip the center of the V you just created with your right hand firmly into the V of the other person's right hand. Don't grip so hard that you crush their hand, and be careful not to hold on too long. If you are greeting someone you already know, consider using both hands, placing your left hand on the person's arm or hand while you shake with your right. This adds warmth and connectedness.

Although handshakes are a common form of greeting in many countries, it is important to recognize that different cultures have various ways of greeting. If you are meeting an international client, be sure to learn the best and most appropriate way to greet them. For instance, in Vietnam people shake both hands vigorously. In Thailand, India, or Cambodia people generally greet another person by putting their hands together (as in a praying position) and sometimes add a bow. In Japan, it is typical to bow, but for those in the UK or France, a handshake will do (in France they may also add a kiss to both cheeks). And in Italy, they kiss twice on each cheek.

In Mexico, typically one kiss on the cheek if you are familiar with the person, but typically for formal or business meetings a handshake is appropriate. Whether it is a firm handshake, a quick kiss on the cheek, a respectful bow or a warm hug, it's important to do your homework and make your potential clients feel at ease. A quick online search for global etiquette and the appropriate greetings for a specific country will reveal the best way to meet someone from another part of the world.[3] Remember, your initial greeting makes a monumental difference in your first impression.

Dress Professionally
In the past few decades, business attire has leaned toward a more casual trend. It started with "Casual Fridays," and then moved to "Dress Down Thursdays," and now for many companies, the informal attire is every day of the week. Granted some businesses encourage a relaxed atmosphere for their employees, helping them to feel comfortable and creative while other businesses maintain standard attire of suits, dresses, coats and ties. As a salesperson, you must dress professionally no matter who you are meeting. You can still be sensitive to the atmosphere of your client's workplace, but generally speaking, it is best for you to be overdressed, rather than underdressed.

Curt is a financial planner in Dallas, where most of his business clients dress in the standard coat and tie. He also has clients in Austin, Texas – a college town, known for their tech and music industries and a city motto of, "Keep Austin Weird." Needless to say, business casual is the norm in Austin, and a person in a business suit is the rarity. What is appropriate in one setting may look a little out of touch in the other. The key is to always look respectable and neat, no matter where you are meeting or with whom. You may also want to consider the time of year and location. When Blake Dinkmeyer had an appointment in Houston in the middle of a hot Texas summer, his client told him, "Don't wear a suit because you are meeting me in a warehouse, and it's 100 degrees in there. I will feel more comfortable if you are casual and not in a suit and tie." So Blake opted for a golf shirt and nice pants instead.

If unsure you may want to call your prospective client the day before to confirm the meeting, and to also ask what would be the most appropriate attire. Keep in mind, your attire sets the expectation for what is going to transpire in the meeting. Dressing with professionalism brings respect and shows that you are there to do business. If you go to a doctor's office you expect to see the doctor in a white coat or scrubs, not a wrinkled shirt and jeans. Furthermore, studies show that when a doctor adds a stethoscope around his neck (even if he doesn't use it), he is generally more respected. That just goes to show you the power of our appearance – its sometimes the little things that matter. Keep in mind, your potential client expects to see a professional when you walk through the door.

Be Early

It is hard to calculate how many sales are lost simply because the salesperson was late and kept the potential client waiting. The Kinder Brothers always say, "If you are not ten minutes early to every appointment, you are late." Ron Price, a good friend and client of the Kinder Brothers and senior vice president, chief marketing officer of American National Insurance Company, often teaches there are only three reasons why people are late:

- They don't care about their time or the prospect's time.
- They are disorganized with their time, demonstrating a lack of discipline.
- Or it is a true emergency, but most of the time that is not the case.

How do you stay on top of your time and ensure that you are always early? We encourage you to plan out your daily schedule carefully, so you give yourself plenty of time to get to the meeting location. We will talk about this in more detail in Chapter Seven. Set the timer on your cell phone to alert you to when you need to leave the office. Add in time for possible traffic or detours. Plan out your navigation the night before, so you have a general idea of how much time you need to get to the different locations you will be visiting throughout your day. Prepare the day before with all the files and tools necessary for your presentation. Decide what you are going to wear the night before your meeting, so you can get up and get going. You may want to set the clock in your home or office ten minutes ahead of time to help push you toward being early. Your promptness is a first step toward a positive encounter and offers a great impression before your meeting even begins.

Impress for Success

Dr. Michael Mescon, dean emeritus of Georgia State University's College of Business Administration, is the author of *Showing Up for Work and Other Keys to Business Success*. He taught his young students who were preparing to go out into the business world, "If you just show up, you're going to have 75% of the people in this world beat. If you show up on time, now you have 90% of the people beat. If you show up on time, dressed, ready to play, you'll have them all beat. That's the way to be successful." Simply put: show up on time, dressed, and ready to engage with your potential clients.[4]

The Kinder brothers have often told the story of the time a salesperson came into their office hoping to sell a new technology system to their staff. Five minutes into the meeting, Jack interrupted the salesman and asked, "Sir, do you want to make a sale today?"

The young salesman immediately replied, "Well, yes sir, I do."

With a direct and stern gaze Jack told him, "If you want to make a sale today, you need to get out of your chair right now, walk into the hallway and throw away the gum you have been chewing since the moment you came in here. And when you come back, stop talking in techno mumbo jumbo jargon. Speak in terms we can understand."

The young salesman jumped up and headed out the door. Jack and Garry waited a few minutes for him to return, but he was long gone! He hopefully learned two important lessons that day: never chew gum on a sales call and use terms your potential client can understand (we'll talk about the latter in Chapter Four). There are certain actions that should be taboo for every salesperson, no matter what industry. Chewing gum, checking your cell phone often and arriving late, are actions that should be avoided at all costs. Remember, you only have a few seconds for your potential client to size you up. It's all about what the client sees before you even utter a word.

The Kinders always say, "You get no second chance to make a good first impression." To make a good first impression, focus your attention on the other person. Be sincere and willing to listen. Be positive and enthusiastic and maintain a posture of confidence. Allow your body language to speak before a word comes out of your mouth. Practice giving the people around you the gift of your smile. The non-verbal keys we discussed in this chapter will enable you to strengthen your connections and create a great first impression. Never underestimate the power of what you don't say.

Recapping the Essentials

Positive Truth:
Make a strong first impression before you say a word.

Positive Discussion:

- Describe a time when someone made either a good or a poor first impression on you. What was it that stood out?

  _____

  _____

  _____

- What is the one area you can improve on when it comes to non-verbal communication? How do you plan to improve in this area?

  _____

  _____

  _____

- Think of the most confident person you know. What is it about their body language that speaks confidence without him or her saying a word?

  _____

  _____

  _____

Positive Actions:
Choose an accountability partner who will be honest with you and has your best interest in mind. It may be a spouse, a colleague or a close friend. Ask them to observe your body language when you are engaged in a conversation with them or another person. Tell them to consider the following and give you their feedback:
- Posture
- Eye Contact
- Hand Gestures
- Smile
- Idiosyncrasies

_____

_____

_____

_____

_____

CHAPTER 2

Presence

Five Secrets to Undistracted Conversations

*Most conversations are just alternating monologues.
The question is, is there any real listening going on?*
LEO BUSCAGLIA

It's the top of the ninth. The bases are loaded with two outs. The pitch is good. The batter hits a high fly ball to left field. It all depends on this catch. All eyes are on the outfielder. And just as he is about to catch the ball…

…he hears a ping on his cell phone and stops to check his message! He misses the catch, the game is over. The opponent wins.

"That's crazy," you say, "That would never happen!" But it does happen every day in the field of conversations. A text, a phone call, a message alert or an email is all it takes to get our eyes off of the game and expose our lack of presence in the conversation. Distractions are an annoyance when it comes to talking with friends or family, but they are a game-changer when it comes to sales and missed opportunities.

Most of us live with a constant flow of distractions that keep us from focusing on the present. For some, being connected to technology becomes a crutch, offering a feeling of importance or productivity. Ironically, as much as we love the devices that keep us connected, they can often be the biggest culprit in keeping us disengaged from the person in front of us. A study by the University of Essex revealed that simply having a cell phone visibly present in the room made people less likely to develop empathy or intimacy during meaningful conversations. Even when no one checked their phone – just having it visibly in the room lowered the level of engagement! Isn't it amazing to think of the power that little device has in our lives and especially over our ability to listen and focus with others?

It takes a deliberate effort to reduce distractions and strengthen our attention. One of the greatest qualities you can demonstrate in sales or in life is the gift of making others feel sincerely important to you. Your ability to be fully present, making your client feel as though they are the most important person in the room, can have a lasting positive impact. When meeting with a client, consider the following ways to eliminate interruptions.

Choose Your Surroundings Wisely. As we mentioned earlier, one of the most important distractions to eliminate when meeting with a prospect or client is your cell phone. Don't just silence your device, put it out of sight. The texts, notices, and emails can wait until you are finished with your conversation or meeting. Additional distractions such as loud noises, television, or other people in the room can also take our focus away from the conversation. Remember; you want your client to be just as attentive as you are, so it is wise to choose a meeting location with as few distractions as possible.

Recently, Karol met a client for lunch at a local cafe. The table was located near the entrance, and Karol's chair faced toward the door. They were seated front and center, in full view of everyone who came into the cafe. Since this was a neighborhood restaurant, Karol was acquainted with most of the people entering the restaurant and felt an obligation to say hello to each of them. You can imagine the depth of engagement she had with her client as they tried to talk together that day.

When choosing a meeting place, consider places that are conducive to conversation and eliminate as many diversions as possible. Sports grills with large, loud televisions are probably not your best location for an important meeting with a client. Make a list of three or four restaurants, coffee shops or meeting places in your area that are typically quiet and uncrowded. In today's world, it is difficult to find a quiet restaurant, so you will need to make a deliberate search to discover one. Schedule as many appointments as possible in pleasant environments which offer optimal opportunities to concentrate and listen to your clients.

Diminish Mental Distractions. Have you ever considered decluttering your mental life? If you have an important email, phone call, or task looming over you, take care of it before you enter into a conversation. The less clutter you have floating around in your mind, the better you will be able to tune into your client. If at all possible, schedule your day so that you take care of the more difficult tasks earlier in the morning, then you will be able to focus on the one-on-one meetings you have with people later in the day. If you clear up those looming loose ends, then you can put your full focus on the person in front of you. It may help to make a list of the activities you still need to complete, since getting it out of your brain and onto paper can help you prioritize and set them aside for later.

You may also want to consider reducing some of the non-essential obligations in your life in order to better concentrate on what is necessary toward reaching your goals. In his book *Essentialism*, author Greg McKeown writes, "Many capable people are kept from getting to the next level of contribution because they can't let go of the belief that everything is important. But an Essentialist has learned to tell the difference between what is truly important and everything else."[5]

When your mind is cluttered with too many non-essential tasks, your concentration will be distorted. Think carefully about all the responsibilities you are juggling and recognize the areas that create a brain tug-of-war when you are attempting to pay attention to another person. Set the non-essentials aside and give your full attention to the person in your midst. The Kinder Brothers often say, "If you are going to be somewhere, be there."

Be an Engaged Listener. Think about a time when you sincerely felt understood. What were the signals that the other person gave you that they were actively listening? As we learned in the last chapter, eye contact makes a significant difference, as well as certain facial expressions. Reflecting the emotions of the person you are talking with can also help someone to feel seen and heard. A raised eyebrow when they are sharing something surprising or a concerned look if they are sharing a problem, can go a long way to reassuring the other person that you are paying attention. You may even give small verbal hints such as "Uh huh" or "Hmmmm," or "Oh I see."

Another way to show that you are sincerely listening is to repeat back to the person some of what you hear them saying. Something like, "Oh I love hearing about….." The best way you can demonstrate that you are really listening to another person is to ask a question that naturally occurs from what they are saying. The danger in trying to come up with questions is that you don't really listen to what the other person is saying, because you are trying to think of the next question or of what you want to say next. But if you make the decision to listen with interest to the other person, natural questions will follow.

Often in sales, it is easy to think we have all the answers that our potential clients need. A person who has all the answers, rarely asks questions. Instead of thinking we know what our client needs or wants, we must recognize that we don't know everything about our client's life and well-being. Think of yourself as an explorer, rather than an expert. As an explorer, you need to discover what makes your client think the way he or she does. What are their interests? What do they value most? Explorers turn the focus on the client, but self-proclaimed experts turn the focus on what they know. An explorer stays engaged in the quest for more knowledge and insight about the client, whereas an expert is disengaged from the client's interests

Many times, when you ask the right questions, the prospect will tell you not only what to sell, but how to sell it. Great salespeople are not necessarily the most proficient conversationalists, but they are good listeners. They ask pertinent questions and pay attention to the responses. A key way to maintain a sense of presence is to listen intently to what your client has to say.

Write it Down. There are times you may become mentally distracted because an important thought pops into your mind, and you want to share it. Instead of interrupting or allowing your mind to wander with what you want to say, keep a pen and pad nearby and quickly jot down a word or two to help you remember the thought, so you can bring it up later. We've been known to scribble thoughts on napkins, coffee shop receipts and business cards. Make sure to have a pen and paper handy at the beginning of a conversation, so you don't need to scramble around looking for it, which would only be an added distraction. The point is to maintain your concentration on what the person is saying rather than on what you want to say next.

Writing yourself a brief note or word can help you maintain your interest in what the other person is saying without forgetting your thought. You may want to explain the purpose for the pen and pad of paper as you place it on the table at the beginning of the appointment. Something like,

"I like to keep this pad handy, so I can listen more intently and record any thoughts that come to mind." This will compliment your client and make them feel as though he or she has your full attention. Garry always carried little blank cards (about the size of business cards) in his suit pocket and simply said, "If you don't mind, I'd like to make some notes about our conversation," as he pulled out the cards.

Use the cards to write down brief, pertinent information you learn from your potential client. When you return to your office, type up the notes that you wrote down from your initial conversation and create a confidential file on the client, so that you can refer to it when you plan to meet again and refresh your memory. You will also want to use small cards to write down referred leads once your prospect becomes a client. It's amazing how small notes written to yourself now can have a big payoff for the future.

Stay on Target with an Agenda. According to a recent Harvard study, adults spend only about 50% of their time living in the present.[6] That tells us that typically both our minds and the minds of our clients tend to wander and become distracted. For many years, the Kinder Brothers have taught a specific technique to insurance salespeople around the world. They call it, "Point to Watch Technique." The concept allows your conversation to stay focused, on topic and on target to make a sale. Here's the idea:

After you have exchanged initial greetings, begin each sales interview by pointing to your watch (or nearby clock) and say, "When we originally set this meeting, I told you it would take 45 minutes, is that still okay by you?"

Next, present a one-page typed agenda to the client and say, "Here's the agenda we're going to follow, but before we get to these, is there anything on your mind that you want to be sure I cover?"

One time, Garry sat down to visit with a potential client, a married couple. He started the meeting with the "Point to the Watch" approach, asking if the timeframe was agreeable. He showed them the agenda and then asked if they had anything on their mind they wanted to talk about first. The wife immediately spoke up and asked several specific questions concerning her 401K. As Garry addressed her questions, the conversation naturally flowed into a big sale. This approach allows the salesperson to honor the client's time but also addresses their needs. It keeps the meeting focused and diminishes distractions.

Karol uses a similar "Agenda Approach" when she conducts team meetings for Engage Parenting Initiative, the non-profit she started. When converging with her executive team for strategy meetings, she sets the timeframe (both a beginning and ending time) and places a typed agenda in front of each team member. There is always a time slot for questions at the end of the meeting, so members know they will have an opportunity to ask questions. Typed agendas keep the meeting on target and moving forward, avoiding distractions.

Face-to-Face Advantage
It's no surprise that the majority of commerce, transactions, and sales in the world today are increasingly handled online. From buying cars to buying clothes and even our groceries, online sales have skyrocketed and will continue to do so. Perhaps you are wondering, *is a salesman's presence important anymore?* Let's reflect back to chapter one for a moment. If ninety-three percent of communication is non-verbal, then when we try to do business online our communication is highly limited. All of the non-verbal cues (eye contact, touch, empathy, voice intonation, etc..) that are necessary for understanding in communication are missing. Granted, for some sales, that's fine. We don't necessarily need to talk with a salesperson when buying index cards or a set of pens or a trash can. But there are certain products that require personal guidance, professional insight, and positive encouragement.

If only seven percent of a presentation comes down to the actual words in the text, then key information is lost when you are sending texts and emails. As the sender, it is important to acknowledge that what you are sending could possibly be misconstrued. Case in point, an experiment in a 2005 study asked the test participants to email ten statements to a recipient with some of the statements being serious and others sarcastic. The senders honestly thought the recipients would correctly identify the intended emotion behind each of the statements. Interestingly, the recipients of the emails only correctly identified the seriousness or sarcasm 56% of the time. That's only slightly better than chance.[7]

Why are texts and emails so easily misunderstood? Often people interpret texts and emails according to the bias they have already formed in their minds. A simple text saying, "Good job," can be misconstrued as slightly sarcastic by someone who struggles with self-confidence or tends to be pessimistic. Unless a thumbs-up or smiley emoji accompanies the words, it is easy to assume the negative. Studies show that given a set of circumstances, most people will defer to the negative and see things from a more critical point of view. If your message is void of non-verbal cues or emotions, then misunderstandings and miscommunication can easily occur.

A 2011 study led by psychologist Bradley Okdie at the University of Alabama demonstrated the powerful difference face-to-face interaction has when it comes to communication. In the study, test participants were divided into pairs and given the instruction to simply converse and get to know the other individual. Some of the participants were told to only communicate through texts; while others were instructed to interact face-to-face. Certainly, face-to-face interactions take more effort because they require active engagement with a live person, but the outcomes were significantly more positive in personal encounters. The study revealed face-to-face meetings received more positive ratings of both the partner's character as well as an overall more enjoyable experience in getting to know them.[8]

Even phone communication loses a measure of implications that face-to-face meetings can strengthen and reinforce. When you are talking to someone on the phone, you can hear voice intonations, but you can't see your client's eyes or facial expressions. When you can't see the visual expressions of a person, it is much more difficult to catch the cues that show they are interested or understand what you are saying. Bottom line, your presence is immeasurably important when it comes to getting your message across. We recognize you can't be in front of your client every time you communicate, but we encourage you to be aware that many of your signals are lost when you depend on technology rather than personal touch.

How do you bridge the gap and make your online communication more effective? Here are a few ideas:

Add Adjectives and Specifics. Instead of saying, "It was good to meet you today," try adding a bit of feeling as well as personalized comments. "I truly enjoyed meeting with you today and was glad to know we share a common interest in hockey."

Be Thoughtful of the Recipient's Interpretation. As much as possible, try to consider different possibilities of how your client may receive the words in your communication. Reread your text or email with their viewpoint in mind.

Be Kind and Considerate. Although you want to be clear and concise in both texts and emails, be careful about being too short or abrupt. Reread your communication to make sure it doesn't come off too blunt or gruff. Add some words that convey feelings and when appropriate, use an emoji or emoticon.

Proofread! Read and reread your communication before you send it. Read once for clerical errors and read it a second time to consider how your recipient may interpret your words. Never email or text late at night when you are tired or have had alcohol or something else that could influence your ability to think clearly.

Make Use of Video Conferencing When Needed. GoToMeeting, Zoom conferencing and RingCentral Meetings are all highly rated and allow you the flexibility to experience live video conversations. Make sure you are proficient in using these tools or they can have a negative effect on your presentation. Be sure to get rid of all distractions or background noises, and again maintain a professional image both in what you wear and with your surroundings.

Obviously, the best way to communicate a clear message is through personal interaction where all the non-verbal cues are present. To reduce misunderstandings and increase connections with our clients, it is imperative to recognize the potential for miscommunication through texts and emails. Wise salespeople build their awareness, strengthen their focus, and stay in tune to the messages they are giving and receiving.

A Fully Present Mindset

One of the deepest human needs is to be understood. If a potential client feels you are actively engaged in conversation and that you "get them," you are much more likely to have a client for life. True connection comes through listening to others and letting them know that they are the most important person in the room. In a distracted culture, your job is to go beyond the norm and make a deliberate effort to practice focused engagement with each person you encounter.

Dr. Emma Seppala, author of *The Happiness Track*, writes, "When you are fully present, you are focused on others rather than yourself. As a consequence, you naturally come across as confident: instead of worrying about what others are thinking of you, you are composed, genuine and natural." Additionally, Dr. Seppala points out that charisma and the ability to be fully present is not so much a gift as it is a learned skill.[9] Instead of making excuses for your distractions, create an intentional plan to reduce the temptations that rob you of focus. Increase your ability to pay attention to others, by making them the priority.

Being present in conversations begins with a shift in mindset – a shift from focusing on your own needs to focusing on the needs of the person with whom you are engaging. It's easy to live in your own world, thinking that your texts or emails or circumstances are more important than the people with whom you are talking. But when you consider others' needs as more important than your own, you develop a new way of thinking. Creating an atmosphere of attentiveness comes from a heart that truly cares about the other individual. Make a decision that you are mentally "all in" with every conversation you encounter.

Recapping the Essentials

Positive Truth:
Make your client feel like the most important person in the room by being present in the conversation.

Positive Discussion:
- Describe a time when you were in a conversation with someone and you knew they were distracted or not listening. What were some of the clues that showed you that they weren't paying attention?

\
\
\

- Why does a cell phone sitting on the desk or table in front of you create a distraction?

\
\
\

- In what ways do you need to improve your attentiveness toward others?

Positive Actions:
Practice attentively listening to a family member or close friend. Set aside a time and a place to meet, and be sure to choose a location with limited distractions. Be an explorer and ask questions that will encourage conversation and allow you to learn something new about the person with whom you are meeting. Your goal is to be fully present and apply the principles you learned in this chapter. Write down your experiences and what you learned. How did you feel after the meeting?

_____

_____

_____

_____

_____

_____

CHAPTER 3

Power Words

Dynamic Communication to Galvanize Sales

> *There may be no single thing more important in our efforts to achieve meaningful work and fulfilling relationships than to learn to practice the art of communication.*
>
> MAX DE PREE

In one of the most stirring speeches ever delivered, Prime Minister Winston Churchill addressed the House of Commons in June of 1940. France had fallen to the German forces, and now Churchill had to present the very real challenges England was up against, garnishing his speech with strength and resolve. His unforgettable words inspired courage and responsibility throughout the world:

> *Hitler knows that he will have to break us in this Island or lose the war. If we can stand up to him, all Europe may be free and the life of the world may move forward into broad, sunlit uplands. But if we fail, then the whole world, including the United States, including all that we have known and cared for, will sink into the abyss of a new Dark Age made more sinister, and perhaps more protracted, by the lights of perverted science....*
>
> *...Let us therefore brace ourselves to our duties, and so bear ourselves that, if the British Empire and its Commonwealth last for a thousand years, men will still say, "This was their finest hour."*

While Churchill was one of the most courageous leaders this world has ever known, his powerful oratory is perhaps one of his greatest legacies. Warren Dockter writes, "Churchill believed, unsurprisingly, in the romantic power of speeches. He wrote that if a man's oratory was powerful enough, he would become an 'independent force.'"[10] Churchill carefully chose his words and used them to paint a picture, inspiring both emotion and action.

Our words matter. They can be used to encourage friends and family to push forward and follow their dreams. But words can also be used to discourage others, making them feel defeated before they even try. Words can tell a story, portray a need, or inspire new ideas. Although we talked about the power of what you don't say (body language) in chapter one, we can't ignore the fact that the words we choose can have a positive or negative impact on people's decisions.

Think about a time when a person's words deeply mattered to you. Most of us can quickly remember the negative impact someone's words had on us, whether it was bullying or discouraging remarks. But hopefully, we can also recall a few positive words that helped us along life's way. In Karol's life, her dad Garry Kinder was a constant source of encouragement. His words pushed her to strive for excellence. Simple phrases such as: "I believe you can do it," or "You've got what it takes," spurred her on to reach her goals in writing and speaking.

In the sales industry, we want to use carefully chosen words for greatest impact. In this chapter, we will not only give you some power phrases but also address wise strategies and methods to get your message across to your clients and prospective clients.

Power Questions

Certain strategic questions can open doors and allow us to make a stronger connection with our clients and prospects. Ultimately, every client wants to be assured that we honestly care about them and their needs. The following questions are suggestions for you to use at appropriate times when initially meeting with a client. An initial question you may want to use when first contacting a potential client over the phone is:

"Hello, _____. Is this a convenient time for you to talk?" This is a thoughtful, courteous and impressive question to ask as you begin the conversation. The first sign of respect you can show to another individual is to say their name (correctly) and show them that you respect their time. Asking if it is a convenient time to talk demonstrates that you care about their schedule. If they answer, "Not really," then you can respond by asking, "When would be a good time for me to call again?" At this point, they may ask, "Well what is this about?" This is your opportunity to introduce yourself and tell them a little about what you do and why you would like to meet. Then continue the conversation by asking, "Would a Tuesday or a Wednesday be best for me to call?" Giving them a choice helps them in making a decision rather than leaving it open-ended.

Of course, they may respond in the affirmative to your initial question saying it is a convenient time to talk, in which case you respond with a polite introduction and explanation of why you are calling. As you sense that they are open to learning more, let them know you would love the opportunity to share about the details and/or benefits of your product or services. Offer several dates when you are available to meet and ask them which of those dates would work best for their schedule.

Once you have set the appointment and are ready to meet, here are some additional questions to help your client know that you have their best interest in mind.

"When we first set this appointment, we said we would meet for about an hour. Is this still okay by you?" Again, this question reassures the prospective client that you respect their time and want to honor the appointment time that was set. You may remember this question from the previous chapter as the "point to watch" question.

"In order to do a good job for you, would you mind if I ask you a few important questions?" When meeting a prospective client in person, your first objective is to get to know them, specifically their needs and desires. You will need to ask several good questions to connect with your client, but first, you want to let him or her know why you are asking. By opening your conversation with this question, you are letting them know in a kind and positive way that you are asking this in order to do the best job for them. In sales, you must recognize that your most important objective is to serve your client and understand their needs. It is not about *your* sale – it is about their need. Always work from the vantage point of serving your client.

"What product (company or line of products) do you currently use?" This question allows you to understand your prospective client's current status. Where do they currently buy? What do they currently own? Certainly, you will want to tailor this question to the type of industry you are in. Here are varied examples of questions you can ask according to your specific sales areas:

- Skincare Line: "What skincare line are you currently using?"
- Car Sales: "What kind of car are you currently driving?"
- Real Estate: "Are you currently working with an agent?"
- Health & Wellness: "Are you currently on a vitamin regimen?"
- Jewelry or Clothing Line: "What are some of your favorite lines of clothing/jewelry?"
- Insurance: "With what companies do you currently have permanent life insurance?"
- These are simply examples. Take a moment to consider the perfect question for your industry.

Write the question on the lines below:

_____

_____

_____

"About how much were you hoping to invest?" When you are planning to make a sale, you need to be aware of what your client is hoping to spend. This will save you time and allow you to zero in on a range of products that are right for your client. Certainly, you can show them a few products above and below their spending threshold, but you will be able to begin at a more accurate level when you ask this question.

"Do you have any questions that I haven't yet covered?" After you have explained your product, one of the next steps is to ask if your prospective client needs more information. Inviting questions opens the door to understanding our client's interests and needs. It's easy to push forward with what we know and what we want to tell our prospective client; but when we stop to listen and address their questions, we learn what we didn't know about our client's thought process, and we move closer to a sale.

"Is there anything else I can assist you with today?" Never assume that once you have made a sale that you are finished selling. There are always possibilities for additional sales and ancillary products. Even if you didn't sell the product you were initially meeting about, you can always recommend different products according to their needs. This question gives you the opportunity to open new doors and find out the further needs of your client. It also stimulates your client's thinking and helps them explore additional possibilities. It is important not be pushy at this point, but simply to open the door for added extras.

"Is there anyone else you know who could benefit from our services (or our product)" Your best opportunity for new sales is personal referrals. If your customer is satisfied with your service or product, you do not want to miss the opportunity to ask for friends or family who may also benefit from your presentation. Even if the person you are meeting with does not buy from you, you can still use this question to stimulate referrals. Every encounter can be a positive encounter for future contacts and prospects.

Without a doubt, well-chosen questions can open up the door to conversation and understanding between you and your prospect. Questions keep you from doing all the talking and help you do more of the listening. Questions enable you to help prospects recognize what they want or discover what they need. Questions crystallize your prospects thinking so that the idea becomes their own. Questions give people a feeling of importance and show that you respect their point of view. When you respect what they have to say, they are more likely to respect what you have to say. Utilize the power of a question to open opportunities and build empathy for others.

Winning Phrases

In the sales world, there are several key phrases that can build client connections and lead to positive outcomes. The following phrases are simple, but powerful examples of ways to express thoughtfulness and strengthen connectedness. Memorize the ones that apply to your business and be ready to use them when appropriate.

I appreciate you taking the time to meet. When we say this phrase during the initial handshake along with eye contact and a sincere smile, we are off to a great start!

I want to make sure I understand what you are saying. This shows the client that first and foremost you want to understand their needs. As you repeat what you heard them saying, it reassures your potential client that you are listening and care about their situation.

I'm happy to assist you. Once you understand your client's needs, then you can point them in the direction they need to go. Instead of telling them what they need, let them know you are happy to assist them and then lead them to the product or service that will benefit them the most.

I'm grateful for the opportunity to do business with you (or serve you). Every person you encounter deserves a thank you, whether they bought from you or not. Thank them for their time. Thank them for their willingness to look at the products or consider the services. Thank them for allowing you to share your ideas or concept with them. When we thank a person, we are building a positive connection with them. When demonstrating the endearing quality of gratitude, your client or potential client is more likely to return again and again. If appropriate, follow up your meeting with a thank you note or email.

I look forward to seeing you again. This implies that you are confident that they will like your product or service so much that they will return again. If you intend to follow up with them, ask, "Do you mind if I stay in touch with you either by email or phone?" It is wise to stay connected with your clients, following up with them at least every few months. The danger in not following up with your clients is that they will possibly be contacted by your competitor in the meantime. A solid connection is typically built with your client when you communicate with them on a regular basis, but not just for a sale. Make it a habit to send out birthday cards and holiday cards. Newsletters, quarterly updates or helpful articles are also great ways to stay in contact.

Keep these winning phrases tucked away in your mind and ready to use when engaging with a potential customer or client. You may find that there are additional keywords that are specific to your industry. Create your own personal list of winning phrases and write them on a small card. Keep your list in a place where you will see them often. Practice saying them, so that they roll off your tongue at the opportune time.

Successful Strategies and Methods

Churchill believed that strong oratory skills were not necessarily a result of natural talent, rather he believed they could be developed. Personally, he didn't see himself as a natural speaker, so he worked hard to hone the craft of speaking. Our presentations may not have a major impact on world affairs as Churchill's did, but they can have a powerful impact on sales. We too must hone our craft and learn communication methods that build a positive connection with clients.

Stories. Stories help connect a client's heart to the product. Often when they hear about another person who benefited from your product or service, they gain a clearer picture of the value. Stories build credibility for what you are offering which motivates potential customers to make a purchase. Always be prepared with several true stories that you can interject in a presentation at the right moment. Practice telling your story in front of a friend or family member to get a feel for the best way to present it.

What is the key to telling a great story? First, know your purpose for sharing it. Make sure the story fits the topic or need you are trying to illustrate. The right story at the right time should fit like a hand in glove to facilitate your presentation. Have a beginning, middle, and end to your story. The beginning should include the dilemma or need that the person was experiencing. The middle of the story should share how your product resolved the dilemma; and finally, your ending should reveal the rewarding benefits that this product has had on their lives. Don't just share facts, but add colorful details to keep the story interesting. The story should be brief and succinctly shared to get the message across without taking away from your presentation or going down a rabbit trail.

Your Story. There is nothing more powerful than sharing your personal story of how you have benefited from your product or service. Potential customers want to know that you believe in the product so much that you have made your own investment in it. Share your story only when it seems to fit into the conversation. Keep it short and to the point, but always remember that no one can argue with your own personal experience.

How do you effectively share your own testimonial? The best personal stories come when we are willing to be vulnerable and share a little insight about ourselves. Begin by sharing your own challenge – maybe it was a difficult circumstance or a mistake or even a crisis. Don't overshare, but simply give a few of the details as to what led you to your need for your purchase. Next, share your "Aha moment" of when you discovered the benefits of your product. And then finally add how your life (your work, your circumstance, etc) is significantly improved as a result of your purchase. Again, keep it short and to the point as you don't want to bore your client with your past.

Positive solutions. Once you have listened to your potential client's interests and needs, it is your privilege to offer solutions through your products or services. Demonstrate or explain why your product offers solutions to their specific interests. You also want to mention that you know other similar products are available, but then share ways your product is unique. There may be a rare occasion when you can see that a product (other than your own) can meet their needs in a better fashion. If possible and appropriate, you may want to recommend the other product. If you are more interested in helping them with their needs rather than making your sale, you will earn their trust and loyalty. Earning your potential prospect's trust is worth its weight in gold and will likely return to benefit you as they recommend you to others.

Facts and Figures. Some people are interested in the facts, figures, and statistics; while others are not. It is important to be equipped with those numbers and ready to answer your prospects' questions. If you sense they are not interested in the numbers, then don't confuse them with too many facts and figures for they will only be mystified. The important thing is to be equipped, just in case you are meeting with someone who loves the data and makes their decisions based on the numbers.

When using facts and figures, make the presentation as appealing as possible. Color, graphs, pie charts, picture graphics all soften the coldness of mere numbers. Don't make it too cutesy, but do consider what would make the most appealing statement to your client.

Intrinsic value. Of course, ultimately your sales presentation should include the intrinsic value of your product or service. What benefit, use, or significance does your product or service bring to your customer? What is it about your product that can meet their need? If applicable, present both the quality and performance to your prospective client. Show the strengths of your product. A comparison study is helpful but should not be the only information you present. Help your potential client understand attributes that make your product worth the investment.

Use words that bring clarity and focus to the value of the product, but always be sincere and truthful in your description. Take a moment right now to write down at least five words that honestly and specifically describe the attributes and worth of one of your products or services.

1. _____

2. _____

3. _____

4. _____

5. _____

Perhaps you used words like reliable, effective, accurate, beautiful, long-lasting, easy-to-use. Make it a practice to make a five-word list for each of the top products you sell. Write them on 3" by 5" cards and review them often so that these words are on the tip of your tongue as you meet with clients. Remember, do not exaggerate the value, but rather tell it like it is. When you use positive words which honestly portray the worth and value of your products, your clients will gain a clearer understanding of your product.

The Five-Minute Difference
The difference between the stars in selling and the mediocre performers is about five minutes. The stars in selling spend five minutes more planning their activity and preparing their presentations. They invest five minutes more in research and study. They put five minutes more in prospecting and contacting potential clients. They are self-disciplined, which makes the difference in the way they communicate with their clients and prospects.

Positive communicators and connectors are:

- **Enthusiastic** – They employ the magic of enthusiasm to inspire others to believe in them and to buy from them. They sell with a sparkle in their eye. They speak with a note of passion in their voice.
- **Resourceful** – They have imagination, initiative, and fresh ideas. They are students who are always looking for the better way.
- **Predictable and dependable** – Their word is their bond, and their acceptance of a challenge is always a forerunner of a job well done. They can always be counted on, never counted out.
- **Courageous** – They stand for what they believe to be right, even in the midst of conflict and criticism. They dare to be an individual whose honor and integrity are respected and admired by all who know them.
- **Persistent** – They believe that "failure comes from following the line of least persistence." Wisely and thoughtfully press forward. One of Winston Churchill's most memorable speeches consisted of only five words, "Never, never, never give up!"
- **Optimistic** – They have a reason for every success, not an excuse for every failure. Continually, they turn the impossible into the possible.
- **Dedicated** – They make a habit of being punctual and following through. Their motto is, "Let me help. How can I serve you?" They are conscientious but never contentious, determined but not dictatorial, dedicated but not demanding.

In this chapter, we have given you power tools to help you build the communication between you and your client or prospective client. Each of the phrases, questions, and techniques are important assets to have in your toolbox when you are meeting with someone. More than likely your company or store has already given you a presentation to memorize. A savvy salesperson is ready with their presentation yet flexible as situations demand. We want to encourage you to consider how these concepts and ideas can fit within your normal sales presentation. If you have the flexibility to formulate your own, then use the power words we have given you to put together a positive approach with your clients.

In closing, we want to give you a few tips that lead toward greater impact. These final reminders are effective for your communication both in sales and in life:

- **Keep your vocabulary razor sharp.** The right word, spoken with emphasis, enthusiasm, and expectancy, becomes your "laser beam" that can melt the granite-like objections of the toughest customer.
- **Be sure you are understood.** In sales, comprehension is key. Words, carefully chosen, properly used, and effectively spoken, can turn a prospect into a client.
- **Keep your words short and simple!** Long, technical words often cause fences and walls to come between you and your prospects. Short, crisp words are far more likely to build bridges of understanding, goodwill and successful sales records.
- **Use words that investigate and motivate.** Avoid words that irritate.

Words that Motivate:
- Congratulations
- Thank you
- Let's
- I would appreciate the courtesy
- I want to make certain I understand
- How can I help
- Please

Words that Build Understanding:
- What is your opinion?
- What do you think?
- Can you illustrate?
- What were the circumstances?
- What do you consider . . . ?
- How do you feel about . . . Could you explain?
- Which would be best for you?

Words that Irritate:
- Understand?
- Get the point?
- Do you see what I mean?
- That's ridiculous
- Bucks
- Deal?
- I, me, my, mine
- You know

Always be aware of the power of your words. Used wisely and enthusiastically, they can lead to solid sales. Like Churchill, hone your craft and be deliberate about the words you use as well as the words you don't use. Most importantly, communicate with sincerity and confidence in order for your clients to know that your words are reliable and trustworthy.

Recapping the Essentials

Positive Truth:
Choice words, communicated in a compelling way, can lead to greater client connection.

Positive Discussion:

- Describe a time in your life when you were moved or inspired by someone's words.

  _____

  _____

  _____

- What are some successful power phrases or questions that you have used when meeting with a client?

  _____

  _____

  _____

- What is one way you can incorporate even a small part of your story into your sales presentation?

  _____

  _____

  _____

Positive Action:

Take time to consider which strategy or method may be most effective in connecting with your specific client base. Prepare a presentation using power questions and phrases along with the strategy or method you plan to use. Write out your presentation, interjecting positive words which accurately reveal the intrinsic value of your product.

_____

_____

_____

_____

_____

_____

CHAPTER 4

Perspective

Observing and Understanding How Your Client Thinks

The most important thing in communication is to hear what isn't being said.
PETER DRUCKER

Born in New York City in 1912, Ben Feldman is considered to be one of the most outstanding salespeople in history. At one point, he held the world record for the most life insurance product sold by a salesman in a career. He has also been noted for the most product sold in a year, and in a single day, with his name appearing in the Guinness Book of World Records. As he neared the end of his career, his annual commission totals were over one million dollars per year, which at that time in history was only equaled by entire sales forces of other insurance companies. He had a lifetime sales volume of over one billion dollars.

Ben was one of nine children, born to immigrant parents Isaac and Bertha Feldman. When his family moved to Ohio, his first sales job was in his family's wholesale poultry business. He started his career in life insurance sales as a young adult. Interestingly, when asked to do speaking engagements, he often refused due to stage fright. He eventually agreed to speak to audiences only if he was interviewed from behind a curtain so he didn't have to view the audience. Despite his fear of speaking on stage, he seemed to have a gift in talking with people one on one and helping them understand the value of life insurance.

He often said that salespeople must learn to listen with three ears. They should listen to…

...What the prospect says.

...What the prospect doesn't say.

...And what the prospect would like to say, but doesn't quite know how to say it.

What made Ben Feldman such an outstanding salesman? In large part, it was his ability to listen beyond what was being said, so he could truly understand his client and explain his product in a way they could comprehend its value. No matter what type of product you are selling, your greatest asset is not only to recognize your potential client's need but also to understand their perspective. One of the ways we can gain a little insight into a prospect's perspective is to understand the different types of buying personalities.

Take for example, Sarah's situation. Sarah needed new tires for her car, so she chose a day to go tire shopping. She fully intended to make a purchase. At the end of the day, her husband asked her, "Did you get your new tires?"

Sarah groaned, "No, I didn't make a purchase today."

Her husband asked, "Well, what happened? Why didn't you buy any tires?"

Sarah replied, "The salesman started explaining all the different tires and the details about each one. After he presented them all, my head was spinning, and I couldn't make a decision. There was too much information, and nothing was clear to me. All I had wanted to do was to go in and buy some new tires. But I walked out confused."

This simple scenario offers a picture of the power of perception. Sure the salesperson was knowledgeable, but he wasn't perceptive. He didn't build a connection or a sale. Why? He was more interested in telling Sarah what he *knew*, rather than listening to what she *wanted*. How do you become a perceptive salesperson? Find out what people want and help them get it. Let's unpack how to understand your prospective client's buying personality.

Comprehending Personality Traits

Although we are each created as unique individuals, we tend to fit into certain personality types. Making a deliberate effort to understand who your potential clients are and how they typically make a decision gives you a greater advantage in making a sale. The tire salesman could have likely made the sale had he taken the time to understand his potential client. Sarah didn't want to be overwhelmed with a myriad of options, she simply wanted someone with field knowledge to direct her to the best tire for her needs. Wise salespeople don't push forward until they have pulled back and considered the personality traits their potential client is exhibiting.

The question is, how do you size up a person you are meeting for the very first time? What are some clues you can tap into to give you a brief but wise assessment? Generally, there are four different buying personalities: the Drivers, the Analyticals, the Amiables, and the Expressives. The Kinder Brothers have taught these personality types for many years as they trained salespeople. Often they divide the audience into four think tanks according to their personality types and send them off to separate rooms. When Jack or Garry went into each room, they typically found interesting shared traits among the people in the room. The assignment for the groups was always simple – find a captain and make a list of top sales ideas. Here's what Jack and Garry usually found as they visited each group:

- The **Drivers** were done and ready to move on to the next item on the agenda.
- The **Analyticals** were looking at the assignment from every angle and complained that they didn't have enough time.
- The **Amiables** were typically still in discussion. Since they didn't want to hurt anyone's feelings, they gave everyone a chance to speak. They were helpful to each other. Most were sitting on the floor or in comfortable chairs just hanging out, not worried about time.
- The **Expressives** were all talking at once and had not yet picked a captain. They were usually having a great time with lots of laughter, but they hadn't made any decisions.

When the Kinder brothers led this exercise in trainings in Asia, they did not understand the language, yet they could distinguish who belongs to which group simply by observing their actions and engagement with one another.

Here are some quick clues to help you identify your potential client's buying personality:

Drivers

Brief Description: need the facts delivered quickly and to the point.

A Driver may exhibit some of the following actions or traits:

- Asks how long this will take
- Looks well-dressed and ready for success
- Glances at watch
- In a hurry
- Has an attitude of "Let's get this done and go on to what is next"
- Makes quick decisions, doesn't want to be bothered by facts or stories
- Wants the bottom line and will make the decision
- Arrives on time and ready to jump into the meeting
- May interrupt or talk over others
- Doesn't want refreshments, just wants to get to the point
- Doesn't like small talk

Physical gestures may include: strong and firm handshake, using large hand motions, crossing arms, putting hands on hips, eye contact, rarely smiles.

Sales Approach to Drivers: Give facts briefly and get to the bottom line quickly. Expect a response immediately. Stay on topic, be clear and concise about your goal. Sincerely compliment them, but don't flatter them.

Analyticals

Brief Description: need time to make a decision and want to make the right decision.

An Analytical may exhibit some of the following actions or traits:

- Asks lots of questions
- Wants to think it over
- Dresses clean, neat and conservative
- Wants to know important details, but doesn't want too many choices
- May want to review details again
- Won't sign documents unless they have read them

- Says, "Let me study this before I agree"
- Wants to know you are honest
- Doesn't like to be interrupted
- Are good listeners, not expressive
- Will arrive to the appointment early
- Speaks slowly and softly

Physical gestures: businesslike but gentle and unpronounced handshake, not expressive, little or no hand gestures or facial expressions, sometimes hard to read.

Sales Approach to Analyticals: Slowly present the basic facts, but don't overwhelm them with too many options or they will become frustrated and confused. Talk softly. Be prepared with answers to their questions, take your time and recognize they will need time to think about it. Give them a deadline to get back with you.

Amiables

Brief Description: relational, polite, compassionate and people-pleasing.

An Amiable may exhibit some of the following actions or traits:

- Cares about your comfort and will often offer refreshments
- Will possibly arrive late
- Loses all sense of time, not in a hurry
- Will notice surroundings
- Dresses comfortably
- Listens more than talks
- May tell stories, also loves to listen to stories
- Demonstrates kindness, compassion and selflessness
- Has trouble saying no, may string you along
- Wants to help you
- May say, "Do you think this recommendation or product is good for me?"
- Speaks in a relaxed and calming way

Physical Gestures include: Gentle and sincere handshake, may offer few arm or hand gestures, may smile or have a relaxed look.

Sales Approach to Amiable: Tell stories and use illustrations, help them feel a part of something bigger. Listen carefully to subtle hints of what they are not saying. Talk gently. Provide clear explanation of your message. They will want to know your recommendation for them.

Expressives

Brief description: delightful, fun, energetic, enjoys laughter and life.

An Expressive may exhibit some of the following actions or traits:

- Likes to talk and tell stories
- Wants to visit before getting started
- Dresses colorfully, fashionably, maybe a little outside the box
- Doesn't want to jump right to the point, wants to share about life
- Typically will be a little late
- May interrupt and speaks loudly
- Often gets off track
- Loves a creative or funny story
- Doesn't care about the facts (the facts just get in the way of the story)
- May exaggerate
- Freely offers compliments

Physical Gestures: Normal handshake (not too strong, not too weak), may want to give you a hug. Uses hands and arms to get point across. Smiles often and maintains eye contact.

Sales Approach to an Expressive: Be prepared to let them talk. Plan more time, so you will be able to have some good warm visiting. Be willing to chat about what is important to them. Talk with animation and humor. Be willing to answer their questions and give them a deadline for decision-making. Give them the big picture rather than weighing them down with details.

No matter with which type of personality you identify, you must be willing to consider the other person's point of view in order to increase the potential for a sale. Take Garry (a Driver) as an example. When someone tries to sell him a product, their best approach is to get the point across quickly, because Garry makes quick decisions. On the other hand, when a salesperson approaches someone like Sarah, an Analytical, they must present their information slowly and be ready to answer her questions because she wants to analyze and digest the information. She buys very slowly and the salesperson must be patient. Karol, on the other hand, is an Expressive and prefers to hear the general overview and learn about the benefits, but asks very few questions about the details. The main point is to follow the sales process, but remember that certain people buy fast, certain people buy slow, and some buy in between.

Honoring the Individual in Each of Us

Although most people can identify with at least one of the buying personalities, it is also important for us to recognize the desire of every person to be thought of as an individual with unique interests and needs. From customizing your own emoji to creating your own brand of wine, our culture is quickly becoming more individualized in nature. We all want to feel seen and heard, and not simply categorized into one of four personality traits. In today's sales world, you will want to recognize the uniqueness of each potential buyer. Keen observations can help you understand your client just a little better – it's listening with that second ear – listening for what they don't say.

Observation means that you are intentional about paying attention to details and processing their meaning. For instance, if you are meeting a potential client for the first time, pay attention to some of the details you notice simply through observation.

If she is wearing bright red shoes, you may surmise that she is creative or has a flair for fun.

If he walks in with shoulders slumped, he may feel slightly unconfident.

If he keeps looking at his watch, he may be in a hurry or have another appointment after yours.

If she has family pictures in her office, you can make an assumption about what she values.

If she only has a picture of her cat, there again you can clue into some of her interests.

If his desk is cluttered, you may ascertain he is either unorganized, overwhelmed or super-busy.

If you see a duck mount in his office, you can safely guess that you are talking with a hunter.

If she has a designer bag, you can surmise that maybe she likes finer, name-brand items.

These are just a few simple examples of putting your observation skills to work. To strengthen your observation skills you may want to put them into action the next time you are eating in a restaurant or waiting in line at a store. Pay close attention to the people around you. Try to notice as many details as you can (without being intrusive) about the people in your midst. Notice their shoes, what they are carrying, how they order, how they carry themselves. What can you learn about the person simply by observing what they don't say? Another fun way to increase your observation skills is to watch a foreign movie without subtitles. Take time to observe the characters and their surroundings and see if you can figure out the characters and discern a bit of the storyline.

Invest your attention wisely by reducing distractions and staying focused. The best observers don't waste time worrying about what people are thinking of them, but rather turn their focus to think about the other person. The more you use your observation skills, the better you become at detecting clues. Use these clues to help you understand the person you are meeting as a unique individual and not simply a type of buyer. Take a genuine interest in them in order to personalize your approach and your presentation. As you observe their interests, you will be much more in tune with how to specifically address their needs.

Being Prospect-Minded

If you listen intentionally, your prospective clients will often tell you not only what to sell to them, but how to sell to them. A wise salesman is a keen observer, noticing clues that reveal both buying personality and information about the uniqueness of the potential client. As we mentioned earlier, Ben Feldman often taught that salespeople must listen with three ears. Listen to:

- What they say.
- What they don't say.
- What they would like to say, but don't quite know how to say it.

Your objective is to listen to what your clients say as they verbally express their interests, needs and wants. But you must also listen to what they don't say by paying attention to non-verbal cues – looking at their watch, crossing their arms, leaning in to catch every detail, etc. As you observe their facial expression, ask yourself if they have a questioning look, a look of understanding or a look like they are ready to move on, or perhaps a look of excitement. What do you notice about them as an individual? What makes them stand apart from other people you know? These signals give you further insight into the uniqueness of the potential buyer.

Finally, an intuitive salesperson pays attention to what their clients may want to say, but just don't know how to say it. You certainly don't want to put words in their mouths, but on the other hand, you do want to help them verbalize their concerns or questions. If you sense your prospect still has some areas that they don't understand or want to talk about, consider using well-crafted questions as we mentioned in the last chapter. Dig a little deeper to get to what they may want to let you know. Here are some additional questions that may help them open up:

- Is there anything that I can help clarify?
- What are some of the hesitations that you are feeling right now?
- What are your initial thoughts on what I've presented so far?
- Are there others who need to be in on the decision process?

Wise questions such as these assist you in listening to your client with a third ear – to hear the things they would like to say but just don't know how to say it. As you open up the discussion, you open up the opportunity for your client to reveal a little more about themselves and their interests, personality traits and needs. Build understanding with the people you encounter. Step into the other person's perspective and be a thoughtful listener. When you listen with three ears, you build understanding and strengthen connectedness leading to long-term relationships with your clients, and you also open the door to new clients.

Consider this illustration from Frank Bettger's, *How I Raised Myself from Failure to Success in Selling*.

While attending a national sales convention, Frank Bettger heard William G. Power, a public relations executive of the Chevrolet Motor Company, tell this story:

I was about to buy a home in Detroit. I called in a real estate man. He was one of the smartest salespeople I have ever met. He listened as I talked, and after a while found out that, all my life, I had wanted to own a tree. He drove me about twelve miles from Detroit and into the backyard of a house in a nicely wooded section. He said, "Look at those gorgeous trees, eighteen of them!"

I looked at those trees; I admired them, and asked him the price of the house. He said, "X dollars."

"What are you talking about?" I said. "I can buy a house just like that for less money."

He said: "If you can, more power to you, but look at those trees – one ... two ... three ... four ..."

Each time I talked price, he counted those trees. He sold me the eighteen trees – and threw in the house! That is salesmanship. He listened until he found out what I wanted, and then sold it to me.[11]

The Kinder Brothers have often said, "The single best source of prospects is personal observation." Once you become prospect-minded, you'll develop a nose for business as keen as the reporter's nose for news. You can develop the habit of paying attention. Most salespeople don't see things; they merely look at them. They listen but do not hear. Keen observation is a powerful mental process and is key to increasing your productivity. It makes it possible for you to evaluate carefully your prospects' problems and to decide upon the best solutions to help them.

Recapping the Essentials

Positive Truth:
Build your observation and listening skills in order to better understand your prospects and clients.

Positive Discussion:

- Which buying personality traits do you most identify with personally?

  _____

  _____

  _____

  _____

- Which buying personality is the most difficult for you to relate to when meeting with a person?

  _____

  _____

  _____

  _____

- How can you bridge the gap of understanding between different personality traits when you meet with a client?

  _____

  _____

  _____

  _____

Positive Action:

Practice listening to your friends and family members with three ears, listening to what they say, paying attention to what they don't say, and also considering what they want to say, but are not sure how to say it. As you make a deliberate effort to listen with three ears, write down a few notes concerning what you have learned about others through the process.

_____

_____

_____

_____

_____

_____

CHAPTER 5

Potential

Boost and Fortify your Sales Expectations

Never underestimate the power of dreams and the influence of the human spirit. We are all the same in this notion: The potential for greatness lives within each of us.

WILMA RUDOLPH

Have you ever made a decision you later regretted? When I was a junior in college, a friend asked me (Karol) to train with her for a marathon. I quickly responded, "Sure, how far is a marathon?" She told me 26.2 miles, and all I could think was, *who in the world runs a race that long? And why?* Despite my misgivings, I somehow agreed and began the grueling training program.

On the day of the race, my family came to encourage me. Most marathoners have a point where they "hit the wall," which is a period in the race when things shift from feeling hard to seeming impossible. Both mental and physical fatigue set in, and the runner begins to entertain thoughts of quitting. When I hit the wall, I needed someone to cheer me on – and that's what my family did! Their enthusiasm gave me the mental boost I needed to finish strong.

Working in sales is much like running a marathon. It's easy to start off with an "I've got this" mentality, but there comes a time when every salesperson hits the wall and feels regret. This is the point where they need a source of encouragement to help them regain a positive mental outlook and help them press on through the tough stuff.

Optimism is essential in sales. In his book, *Barking Up the Wrong Tree*, author Eric Barker wrote, "While you may think the key to being a good salesperson is people skills or being extroverted, research shows that salespeople can be hired based on optimism alone. Researchers found that insurance agents who scored in the top 10 percent of optimism sold 88 percent more than the most pessimistic tenth."[12]

There's a lot to be said for mental fortitude and a positive outlook! At Kinder Brothers International we often say, "Expect the best from yourself and from the people around you." You must train yourself to be at your best every day: mentally, physically and emotionally. But how do you live with great expectations day in and day out when things get tough? How do you overcome the disappointment of rejection and look for the next opportunity?

You begin by changing your mindset; turning your thoughts from dwelling on the frustrations or negatives to thinking about the potential and positives. When you face rejection, you can grieve the loss for just a moment, but then start going in a new direction. Step forward. We suggest keeping uplifting and motivating books (like this one), newsletters, and podcasts close at hand; so you will be ready to infuse your mind with positive thoughts. This encouragement will help you turn from focusing on the negatives and instead help you have a more positive, hope-filled attitude.

Remember, everyone who is successful in sales will have some down days. People will disappoint you. Even the greatest salespeople experience frustration. The good news is the longer you are in the business, the fewer rejections and turndowns you will experience. Even Babe Ruth, one of the greatest homerun hitters of all times, not only broke the record for the most home runs in 1923, but he also struck out more than any major league player that year. You are not alone. Keep in mind, each rejection you face brings you closer to your next sale.

One way to help you face those down times is to have a mentor in your field of sales. When you face a challenge, get in touch with your mentor. Most likely, your mentor will be able to tell you about a bad day that he or she recently had, and yet they somehow got back out there. Think about what you would tell another person who is having a rough time. What words would you use to encourage them? Tell those words to yourself.

Write down some of your favorite motivational statements on small cards and keep them handy. You can pull them out and read them in between interviews, particularly those that are not successful interviews. Below are five motivational statements you can write down on small cards or type into your cell phone notes:

- I can do this!
- Every day in every way, I am getting better and better.
- Persevere! Each hurdle makes me wiser and stronger.
- The harder I work, the better I get.
- Every rejection leads me one step closer to a sale.

Now come up with a few more motivational statements of your own and write them here:

_____

_____

_____

_____

Quitting in the Phone Booth

At a certain point, early on in Garry's career, he was discouraged over sales frustrations – people hanging up on cold calls, people rejecting his sales pitches and people not answering the phone. Some people didn't show up for appointments or canceled the appointment, claiming they just weren't interested in buying life insurance right now.

Garry was ready to throw in the towel, but he was concerned about his brother Jack, who hired him into the business. Garry thought about the effect his departure would have on his fellow sales team. Still, he carefully planned out how he would approach his general manager to tell him that he was going to quit.

At that time cell phones didn't exist, but telephone booths did. Since Garry lived 30 minutes away from the office, he found a private phone booth on his side of town and away from everyone at the office. He had his script written out and was ready to give his notice. He dialed the number and told the administrative assistant hello and asked to speak to his agency manager.

As he waited for the manager to get on the line, Garry became increasingly nervous while he looked over his newly crafted script. When the manager finally got on the phone, Garry heard these words, "Hello Youngster, do you know how good you are? You're one in ten million! That's how good you are! In any event, what's up?"

Garry immediately tore up his script and changed his tone. He simply responded, "Oh I just wanted to know how things were going at the office." Garry went back to work and made a goal that he was going to accomplish a certain amount of sales or get out of the business. He ended up doubling the amount of sales he had been making. Through prayer and hard work, he persevered. Within nine months, he was the youngest agent in Illinois to qualify for the Million Dollar Round Table.

What made the difference? The power of encouragement from someone who believed in him. Do you have cheerleaders in your life? Surround yourself with people who will give you specific and sincere boost of courage through their words. We all need people who are for us, cheering us on when we do well, and cheering us up when we feel discouraged.

Don't walk away from negative people – run! You don't need to be around negative and discouraging people. Certainly, you want people to be honest with you, but you also need people who choose to believe the best in you and will encourage you along the way.

Make Every Occasion a Great Occasion

Live with the attitude of making every occasion a great occasion. In other words, every obstacle, rejection, or interruption can be an opportunity to strengthen your skills, learn, and move forward. Every situation you encounter can be a growth experience. Even the negatives can be transformed into what we call a great occasion. How? Simply by viewing the event through the lens of an expectant, creative, and positive perspective. Ask yourself, what can I learn from this? How can I grow from this? How can I work around this obstacle?

Consider Gretchen's story. It was going to be a big day for her as she had an appointment with one of her better prospects, and she was well prepared. Being new in sales, she was anxious to make a nice commission that day. She arrived early to the prospective client's office and was feeling quite confident in both her appearance and approach. When she let the receptionist know that she was there, her great expectations were dashed as she heard the painful words, "Oh didn't he call you and tell you that he had to cancel?"

This is a scenario that is familiar to most salespeople in one form or another. Disappointments, great and small, happen on a regular basis in the sales world. It's not the size of the disappointment that matters, but the ability to turn and continue to see potential for more sales in new and different directions. Fortunately, as we said earlier, the longer you are in the sales world you will most likely have fewer cancellations and rejections because you will be talking to people who are already clients and you will be getting more referrals.

Was Gretchen's situation a great occasion? Hardly! But wait! Turn that temporary "rejection" into a reward. Many times good results will be found even in these cancelations. There is always a possibility that the very same client who canceled will feel an obligation to do business with her and to give her referrals. Does this happen every time? No, but quite often it is the case that you can build a strong client relationship with those who have to cancel, so don't give up. Gretchen could mention to the receptionist to inform her prospective client that she will be calling in the morning to reschedule.

One thing Gretchen could do with her newfound extra time is to begin calling some of her best prospects that she hasn't yet contacted. Are there any who are located in the same building or neighborhood? What about some of her current clients? She could stop by and say hello to strengthen her connection. Who knows, maybe a client or prospective client will be available to visit. In sales, you need to be ready with back-up prospects in your phone or briefcase, so you can use those little slots of time that open up.

Remember this truth: There are always other sources. There are always other prospects, customers, and clients. The salesperson who realizes this will inevitably grow from anxiety to confidence, from fear to courage, and from pessimism to productivity.

Winston Churchill said, "Continuous effort – not strength or intelligence – is the key to your potential." And we would add the key to your sales success. You must continually stay in front of prospects; you'll win some and lose some, but keep on going!

Depending on our attitude, challenges and obstacles can:

- be viewed as sources of irritation or opportunities for service
- be viewed as moments lost or experiences gained
- be viewed as time wasted or horizons widened
- annoy us or enrich us
- get under our skin or give us a shot in the arm
- monopolize our minutes or spruce up our schedules

No occasion is a "little" occasion. No moment is insignificant in its own way. No person is unimportant in his/her own eyes. Always consider what you can do, instead of focusing on what you can't do or what didn't happen. There are opportunities waiting to be discovered within every disappointment or change in plans. It all comes down to your outlook and ability to see the potential.

Harold Sherman wrote a book entitled, *How to Turn Failure into Success*. In it, he provided a "Code of Persistence" which is especially helpful for salespeople. Consider rewriting this to fit your own sales work and then re-read it often to remind you to persist when you feel like throwing in the towel.

1. I will never give up so long as I know I am right.
2. I will believe that all things will work out for me if I hang on until the end.
3. I will be courageous and undismayed in the face of odds.
4. I will not permit anyone to intimidate me or deter me from my goals.
5. I will fight to overcome all physical handicaps and setbacks.
6. I will try again and again and yet again to accomplish what I desire.
7. I will take new faith and resolution from the knowledge that all successful men and women have had to fight defeat and adversity.
8. I will never surrender to discouragement or despair no matter what seeming obstacles may confront me.[13]

Success in life depends on your willingness to never give up. The reward is frequently delayed, but persistence eventually wins.

Seeing Potential in Objections

Two factors will determine your success in meeting resistance and overcoming objections: attitude and strategy. As with any part of the selling process, strategy can be learned and mastered through practice. But, first, it's important to develop an attitude that puts negative responses in their proper perspective. All too often, pushbacks from the prospect can be viewed as major obstacles to closing the sale. When you develop skills in handling them, you'll find counterpoints can be a welcome part of the sales process. In fact, often the toughest prospect to sell is the one who gives you too little or no feedback because it is hard to tell where he or she stands.

The same applies to the prospect who appears to agree with everything you say because you assume they understand everything about the product. Therefore, the right attitude toward questions and doubts is to welcome them. Once you have the right attitude toward objections, you can develop a strategy for handling them effectively. But to do so, you must first determine whether they are genuine or insincere. The insincere objection, known as sales resistance, is generally illogical and cannot be answered. It's expressed in alibis, excuses, or stalls. The prospect may give you fictitious reasons to hide the real, genuine objection – for example, "Your product has a lot of merit, but I'd like to think about it"; or "I'd like to shop around and do some comparing."

By contrast, the genuine objection has the ring of truthfulness. Here, the prospect feels there's a valid reason for not buying at this time. Examples: "The need is an obvious one, but I have some bills I must handle first." Or, "Frankly, I feel as though I can invest my money better in my own business." Or even, "It's just too expensive for me right now, there's no way I can afford it." These challenges are not excuses. They are honest doubts in the prospect's mind, and you can handle them. As you gain experience, it will become easier for you to distinguish between genuine and insincere objections.

No matter how skillful you become at anticipating and answering questions and concerns before they come up, some will still surface. You can choose to defer these by simply acknowledging their worries and asking permission to answer it later. When you delay an objection during the presentation, you rob some of its potential strength. Also, the delay keeps you on track. Best of all, delaying an objection often "tables it" permanently.

As you move to the closing of your presentation and a genuine question or concern surfaces, you must answer it to the prospect's satisfaction. To hesitate or be evasive may magnify the issue in the prospect's mind and block the close. Confidence of your personal selling power derived from having a strategy for handling obstacles is an invaluable asset. Once your strategy is mastered, you'll be able to remain poised and react calmly when confronted with challenges to the sale.

One strategy for handling concerns or questions begins with the statement, "Let me make sure I understand your hesitation." Then repeat what they have verbalized as their concern. This reassures the prospect that you listened to them and really heard what they are saying. Then address their apprehensions head on. It is wise to create your own list of possible objections before you ever start meeting with clients and to think carefully about the most accurate way to respond to these potential challenges to a sale. This preparation beforehand is invaluable and will help you in confronting possible roadblocks.

Certainly, we cannot foresee every possible objection, but keep in mind we can always respond with hope. Phrases like, "Let's see if we can find a way to …" Or consider this response, "If you really believe in what we are talking about here (this product, or service), then we can find a way to make this work for your situation." You may also want to point out the importance of not waiting to buy. For instance, in the insurance world, if you wait too long, you risk having a health issue in years to come which may increase your premiums or make you ineligible for certain kinds of insurance.

You might want to keep a record of objections raised by prospects, noting how often the initial objection is the real objection. You'll get better at determining which objections are the real ones and which objections just sound good.

The Power of a Made-up Mind

Dr. Edward Rosenow, a renowned surgeon at Mayo Clinic, established his purpose in life and sealed his commitment to medicine when he was just a small boy living in Minnesota's north woods country. One night, he says, his younger brother became quite ill, and the family gathered together, waiting nervously until a doctor could be located.

When a doctor finally arrived and examined the sick boy, young Edward's eyes were riveted on the anguished faces of his parents. At last, the doctor looked up, turned to the parents, and said, "You folks can relax now. Your boy is going to be all right."

Edward, then just eleven years old, was so impressed with the change the doctor's words brought to his parents' faces that he later said, "I resolved right then that one day I would become a doctor, so I could spend my life putting that same light in other people's faces."

There are few experiences more rewarding than putting light in other people's faces. People in sales can know that same type of joy. It is a reward for the salesperson who becomes thoroughly imbued with the value of the contribution he or she makes in their client's life. Whether you are in real estate, product sales or financial services, you have the potential to make someone's life better and brighter.

When you are confident in what you are selling and your ability to sell it, you discover a worthwhile purpose in meeting your prospects' needs and satisfying their expectations. Believe in yourself, your products, and your mission. When you do, you will find that you consistently achieve superior results.

High achievers in all fields understand the power of the made-up mind. They are so dedicated to what they are doing that they can't wait to go to work every morning. Their focus is bringing light to people's eyes. They are thrilled when they help people accomplish what they want and are satisfied with what you brought them.

One of the greatest rewards for sincere salespeople is to hear the words, "Thank you for helping us make this purchase." You may not get that comment every day of the week; but when you are genuinely helping others, you will get it quite often.

Concentrating on the Potential

Selling power originates from developing and maintaining a mindset that sees the potential. The strength of your mindset determines the attitudes you develop about selling and the habits you develop for spending your time. "Thinking right" will move you to join the salespeople who get to the top and stay there.

Make these tenets a dominant part of your thought life:

- **BELIEVE** that the modern-day client is better educated because of the amount of information available online.
- **BELIEVE** that your products and services, properly sold, are of considerably more value to your buyer than any commissions you can possibly earn.
- **BELIEVE** that you are your most important customer. You must be sold on your job, your products, and your ability to perform.
- **BELIEVE** that you should set realistically high goals and achieve them <u>on schedule.</u>
- **BELIEVE** that honest, intelligent effort is always rewarded.
- **BELIEVE** that the customer is most important and must feel understood.
- **BELIEVE** that the power of your sales presentation will always lie in its simplicity.
- **BELIEVE** that almost all development is, in fact, self-development.
- **BELIEVE** that staying physically fit and eating a healthy diet is a prerequisite for maintaining a high level of energy.
- **BELIEVE** that top producers are ordinary people with an extraordinary determination to make every occasion a great occasion.
- **BELIEVE** that your image of yourself determines how far you will go in earning money, gaining clients, and achieving influence.

Study these philosophies. Digest them. Make them a dominant part of your selling strategy, and you will find yourself among those salespeople who go to the top and stay there! Never underestimate the power of concentrating on the potential. Make up your mind that what you sell is valuable and that what you do can make a positive difference in the lives of others. Bring light to your clients' faces by bringing them the good news of what you have to offer.

Be Enthusiastic

Enthusiasm is at the foundation of all progress! Talent is valuable; but, without enthusiasm, it pales at the point of sale. Enthusiasm is the difference between mediocre and superior success in selling. Where do you get this energizing quality of enthusiasm? How do you maintain it after you tap into it?

First, we recommend taking responsibility for your own level of enthusiasm throughout the selling day. Don't leave it in the hands of others or with the circumstances around you. Learn what creates enthusiasm for you. Then, do it – turn it on!

What are your first thoughts when you start a new day? Do you remind yourself of the good news or do you focus on the bad? Begin each day with a grateful heart. There's always something to be thankful for:
- I have a high level of energy – that's good news!
- I have a mind that is alert – that's good news!
- I have challenging work to do – that's good news!
- I have a strong market with great potential – that's good news!
- I'm creating my future today – that's tremendous!

Additionally, we encourage you to act as if you have enthusiasm, even when you don't. Psychologists have concluded that it is easier to act your way into a new way of feeling than it is to feel your way into a new way of acting. Read that statement again. Think about it. It translates to this: Act as if you feel enthusiastic and you will feel enthusiastic. Enthusiasm reflects confidence, spreads good cheer, raises morale, inspires associates, and generates loyalties. It draws customers to you like a magnet. Enthusiasm is contagious.

When you live with a personal enthusiasm that spurs you on each day, you can accomplish great things. Don't be fake or fluffy. Be honest, but uplifting. When you are, you will most likely find that your clients can't wait to meet with you, and they will be much more willing to introduce you to their friends and co-workers. People would rather be around others who pull them up instead of drag them down. In life and in sales, a genuinely positive attitude is an attractive quality, so keep looking up and see the potential!

Recapping the Essentials

Positive Truth:
Believe in yourself, believe in what you are selling and believe in the potential to benefit your prospective client.

Positive Discussion:
- Describe a time when you faced an obstacle and felt like quitting. What helped you get back in the game?

- What is one motivational statement you tell to yourself or share with others?

- When a client cancels, what are some things you can do to fill that time in a productive way?

Positive Action:
Think about people in your life who need a good word of encouragement. Be a cheerleader for them by either calling them or sending them a note or text with sincere and specific words that will give them a boost of confidence. As you lift up others, you will be uplifted as well. Take deliberate action today to build up someone else and help them see their own potential.

CHAPTER 6

Preparation

Peak Performance Doesn't Just Happen

Plan your work for today and every day, then work your plan.
MARGARET THATCHER

An unlikely quote hangs on the wall in the locker room of the San Antonio Spurs basketball team. The author of the quote is Jacob Riis – a social reformer, writer, and photographer from the early 1900s in New York. What words of wisdom could this particular man possibly have said to inspire one of the most successful teams in the NBA? Here's the quote the players see as they prepare to go on the court:

> *"When nothing seems to help, I go and look at a stonecutter hammering away at his rock, perhaps a hundred times without as much as a crack showing in it. Yet at the hundred and first blow it will split in two, and I know it was not that last blow, that did it – but all that had gone before."*[14]

These rich words serve as a constant reminder that what happens in the game is a result of myriad hours of hard work and practice before the game ever begins. Great sports teams don't just happen. The players devote time, energy and sweat through rigorous practice and daily habits to perform at their best on the court or the field or the stage. In sports and in life, spectacular achievements are always preceded by unspectacular preparation. A salesperson is no different. The hours you devote to planning and preparation are the catalyst that leads to your success in front of your prospect. Zig Ziglar always said, "You were born to win; but to be a winner you must plan to win, prepare to win, and expect to win."

The Myth of the Natural

Perhaps you have heard someone say, "He is just a natural-born salesperson." But does selling really come naturally, or is it a result of preparation and perseverance? Granted, some innate qualities make it seem as though a person is a super-salesperson, but could it be that most of their strengths are learned rather than simply instinctive? Consider some of the world's most outstanding athletes. Studies show that some of these elite athletes were not necessarily born with an inherent ability, but have become great as a result of their hours of practice, strong coaching and a never-give-up attitude.

Michael Phelps is one of the greatest swimmers of all time with twenty-three Olympic gold medals to prove it. Certainly, his stature and physical make-up gave him an advantage, but it was his commitment to the unspectacular hours of training both in and out of the water that made him a success. Phelps' training schedule was typically six hours of swimming per day, six days per week, along with lifting weights for an hour and stretching for an hour three days per week. Although he makes swimming look easy, it's not only his natural ability but rather his persistence in practice that turned him into a champion.[16]

In sales, a person may have certain personality traits that allow them to interact well with others, but what makes a top-notch salesperson? It's the hard work no one sees – studying the products, making the calls, preparing for the presentations, and a willingness to learn – that actually bring about the best results. Many great personalities are at the bottom of the sales ranks. It's not simply personality that makes a successful salesperson, it is the unspectacular preparation and perseverance that determines success.

As we said before, successful results are always preceded by unspectacular practice! It takes discipline and determination to do the hard work of preparation. We encourage you to get up early in the morning and practice your pre-approach or script every day. Memorizing takes time and hard work, so don't give up! If you review your script every day for 21 days, it will start to become part of your long-term memory, and you will soon reap the benefits of your hard work.

Prepare Logically – Adapt Needfully

Along with careful preparation also comes the ability to adapt to the circumstances or needs of your potential client. Study the word PLAN.

Kinder Brothers uses the acronym to mean:

Prepare
Logically and
Adapt
Needfully

In other words, make thoughtful, definite plans. Then, adapt and modify those plans as the situation might require.

Great salespeople, like effective performers in all walks of life, are those who are organized, flexible, and adaptable. They size up situations; and when the occasion demands, they quickly, effectively, and confidently alter their original course and go to "Plan B." In the Navy, this kind of adaptability is referred to as "changing the course." In Boy Scout training, it's called "improvising." In football, it's termed "calling an audible." In selling, it's adapting the prepared agenda to meet the need. In other words, the situation is the boss.

In every sales encounter, you must learn to adjust and adapt. When the prospect starts making objections and offering resistance, "call an audible" – adjust and adapt. Display flexibility. Move ahead to achieve your goal, the goal of another satisfied customer. Remember, that in order to be able to adapt needfully, you must be prepared. Ad-libs are for amateurs. Preparation will give you the confidence to adapt, should the situation require it.

One of the key components of planning is wise preparation. Simply put, preparation in sales comes down to these three basics:

- Know your product
- Know your script
- Know your prospective clients

Let's examine each one a little closer:

Know Your Product – No matter what you are selling, whether it's auto parts or commercial real estate or medical supplies, you must become overwhelmingly familiar with what you sell. Study the product; get information from people who are experts in the field. Listen to stories of satisfied customers and find out why they are pleased with the product or if there are any negatives of which to be aware. Study the competition, study the reviews online, get to know both the downsides and upsides of your product.

Know Your Script – Memorize it, professionalize it, personalize it. If you do what comes naturally, you are going to naturally fail. That's why you must know your presentation. Actors on a stage cannot simply show up for the performance. They must have their lines memorized and ready to present to the audience. It may take hours of practice to know your script, but the goal is to know it so well that it rolls off your tongue without having to think about it. It should become second nature

Know Your Clients – Get to know not only the needs but also the interests and priorities of your clients. Be aware of what is important to them. In addition, consider becoming more involved in your community. Be active in your religious organizations, your country club, and your city, so you can build relationships beyond simply work. People like to do business with people they know from the same organizations. Civic, Rotary, Lions, Book Club and other groups can be a great investment of your time.

Twelve Positive Habits of the Pros

Effective planning comes down to creating new habits. When you study the habits of the highly successful professionals in the sales world, you will discover some common practices. Consider these twelve habits that the pros form in order to create sales success.

1. **Wake up employed.** By this, we mean to wake up each day with a sufficient number of appointments set on a favorable basis which allows you to be successful in your business. When you complete a sale, tell the client that you're going to follow up on an annual basis. "Let's go ahead and make that appointment now for (date next year)." That's one appointment that you will have next year. If you have 75 new sales this year, that's going to give you 75 clients to see next year to conduct an annual review.

2. **Believe in total preparation.** Total preparation is critical in the selling process. In most instances, you only have one opportunity to sit down in front of a client and make a sale. You must always

be totally prepared to ask the right questions and be able to answer questions. You want to facilitate the interview, so the client feels very comfortable with you and will buy from you.

3. **Picture yourself as a problem-solver.** By this, we mean that you as the salesperson will not only listen to the prospects need but will also show them a solution that will take care of these needs. For example, in the real estate business, your potential client may say that their house is too small or too expensive; so your job is to lead them to specific solutions that will solve their need. If you sell medical equipment, always keep in the forefront of your mind, the needs you are meeting through your product. View yourself as a problem solver.

4. **Hone probing and listening skills.** As we mentioned in chapter four, sharp listening skills are critical in today's environment.
   - 90% of selling is showing up on time.
   - 110% of selling is showing up on time and being prepared.
   - 200% of selling is showing up, being prepared, and being able to ask the right questions so as to be able to be a problem-solver for your client.

5. **Give the buyer something to say "Yes" to.** This is a great sales technique. Take the example of a salesperson at a fine clothier. She could ask, "Is there anything in particular that you came into the store for today?" Or a real estate agent could ask, "Is there a particular type or size of house for which you are looking?" It is always good to create questions you can ask which give the buyer an opportunity to respond with "yes." Write some possible questions appropriate for your industry in the lines below.

_____

_____

_____

6. **Sell what you own.** If you are the proud owner of your own product, it is much easier to sell to your prospect because you can give a firsthand account of why it is beneficial to your life. No one can argue with your own story; that's why your personal testimony as a satisfied customer speaks volumes.

7. **Narrow your focus.** Concentrate on those problems the individual has mentioned to you. Remember, you can help in so many different areas, but you need to find out what the client wants and needs and then focus on that particular situation. It can confuse a client when you are trying to span too much territory and provide an overwhelming amount of information. You may have a plethora of facts hidden in your head, but you don't have to share it all. Narrow down to what is needful and necessary.

8. **Leverage your key skill.** Each one of us has certain skill sets that come naturally or that seem to stand out among others. If you are a great conversationalist and are gifted at making people feel comfortable during the sales presentation, you should leverage that skill to become a better salesperson. If you are better on the phone, then use that to your advantage. Some people are better in person; while others have a strong phone presence. Build on your strengths and manage around your weaknesses.

9. **Don't waste time with those who waste your time.** This is a great time management tool. We have to concentrate on the fact that we are there to solve the problems of the client. You will find certain people are not interested in buying anything, but they sure would like to get as much information from you as they can without spending any money. You may need to set boundaries with those people who want to simply use you for your insight or knowledge of a product but never plan to buy. Don't ignore those who want to drain you, but don't allow them to keep you from using your time productively either.

10. **Be determined to be the best in your field.** This means that you're going to have to work very hard at learning your business and also learning the communication business. Remember, we are in the communication business; and the better we are at that, the more we're going to be able to help our clients reach their goals. Be a learner, always growing and taking in new ideas in your field and in the fields of technology and communication.

11. **Become influential.** When you are among the best in your field you're going to become very influential in your marketplace. It is important to have credentials if possible in your industry. If there is an additional certification in your field, make a point to achieve this additional credibility. Write articles for local newspapers, participate in radio interviews and podcasts, or speak at local events in your community. Get copies or reprints to share with your clients and prospects.

12. **Take 100% responsibility for your results.** You are in a results-oriented field, so you need to take 100% responsibility for the results that you achieve, whether good or bad. Ask questions and consider what are some of the underlying factors of either your strong sales numbers or your poor ones. Learn and grow from your results, but never allow them to make you prideful or discouraged.

Keep working to develop habits that increase your professionalism and value to your clients. Stewart Johnson put it this way, "Our business in life is not to get ahead of others but to get ahead of ourselves - to break our own records, to out-strip our yesterdays by our today; to do the little parts of our work with more force than ever before."

Confidence and Practice

Confidence and practice go hand in hand. Commercial Real Estate Broker Randy Potts tells the story of a memorable moment in Houston, Texas as he watched Garry demonstrate both the power of preparation and the strength of believing in the possibilities. After Garry spoke at a meeting which Randy was attending, most of the attendees gathered for an afternoon round of golf. As the teams finished, many of the players congregated around the 18th green to cheer (or possibly heckle) the incoming players. Randy remembers standing with his friends and colleagues, watching Garry make his approaching shot to the green.

Unfortunately Garry's ball fell far short of the hole and he was facing a long and difficult putt. With the small gallery standing around the green, Garry smiled at them and examined the green from every angle. Then, much to everyone's amazement, Garry declared, "I'm going to make this putt." Randy and the others shook their heads in disbelief, thinking there is no way for Garry to sink this one. It looked nearly impossible.

Garry persisted, "You just watch. I'm going to make this!" His courageous confidence couldn't be deterred despite the skepticism of the onlookers. Garry took another calculated gaze at the green and then made the move. There was a lot of hooting and hollering as the ball made it left and right and over several undulations and slowed down to a crawl and barely lipped out. It wasn't so much as to whether he made the putt, but rather that he demonstrated the possibility. It was close enough to muster everyone's attention and applause. They stood amazed not only at Garry's confidence but also his accuracy.

Although it has been many years since that inspiring moment, Randy still reflects on that golf game and the confidence Garry exhibited against great odds. How could Garry have such boldness to believe he could make the putt? Practice and preparation. He had practiced and played similar strokes over and over again. Making this putt wasn't just a onetime fluke; it was a result of countless hours of practice and years of playing the game.

Confidence without practice is often based on shallow pride or arrogance. Practice without confidence may get you a little further, but confidence built on the solid foundation of preparation and practice are a winning combination. Allow your hours of practice to strengthen your personal belief that you have the potential to make the sale.

And Then Some!
Emmitt Smith was an All-Pro running back for the World Champion Dallas Cowboys. His impressive statistics are well known to football fans: Emmitt often led all rushers in yardage gained, yards per carry, and touchdowns scored. Little known, and seldom talked about, is what the football experts, like John Madden, called Emmitt's most impressive statistic. *It's his YAC numbers – Yards after Contact.* You see, Emmitt is one of those "And then some" performers. He's at his best after the initial resistance. Emmitt is a model of excellence on this score for everyone in selling to emulate.

We're convinced those three little words, *And Then Some,* make the difference between average salespeople and top performers. Long before the famous discovery by Alexander Graham Bell, a German schoolmaster named Wilhelm Reiss, constructed a telephone through which he could whistle or hum. However, the gadget couldn't transmit speech. Something was lacking! Reiss never let the electrodes touch in his telephone. Bell then followed Reiss and discovered that a little screw controlled the telephone electrodes, allowing the machine to transmit speech.

Accidentally, he moved the screw one-thousandth of an inch and articulate and clear words came through. History records that a fraction of an inch made an enormous difference. You may be just a short distance from success in your selling career. Just a little improvement in your daily planning, a little adjustment in your sales presentation, a little additional product knowledge, a little more positive action, or persistence and unusual success can become yours. Plan and prepare purposefully, proceed positively, pursue persistently.

Chances are good a very slight improvement in your day-to-day selling habits will have a huge, cumulative impact at the end of your year. "It is but the littleness of man that sees no greatness in trifles," said Wendell Phillips. The doors of achievement open wide for the salesperson who sees infinite possibilities in the insignificant. This is especially true with those sales reps who are determined to deliver a little extra and do a little extra. Consider three little words. They will point you toward success. The three words are – And Then Some.

We're convinced these words make the difference between average salespeople and top performers.

The high achievers do what is expected...
And Then Some.

They hold themselves responsible for higher standards.
They make good on commitments and responsibilities ...
And Then Some.

They can be counted on to represent the company
and themselves in a professional manner. Their selling
success secret is wrapped up in these little words...
And Then Some!

Recapping the Essentials

Positive Truth:
Unspectacular preparation creates the opportunity for spectacular sales results.

Discussion Questions:
- What are some of the habits you have formed in your life that help you to be prepared to meet a prospective client?

  _____

  _____

  _____

- Why is it important to adapt and be flexible in your presentation?

  _____

  _____

  _____

- What is one small habit or action that you can do to "go the extra mile" and then some in your business?

  _____

  _____

  _____

Positive Actions:
Memorize your sales presentation and practice sharing it with at least three people. They should be friends or family members who have your best interest at heart and want to see you succeed. Ask them to role-play with you, so you can also practice with different responses. Most importantly, ask them for their honest feedback and welcome any suggestions they want to give you. Remember, there is always room for improvement. We can always learn and grow.

_____

_____

_____

_____

_____

_____

CHAPTER 7

Purpose

Pursuing What Matters Most

When you discover your mission, you will feel its demand. It will fill you with enthusiasm and a burning desire to get to work on it.

W. CLEMENT STONE

The legendary miniseries Lonesome Dove portrays the story of two retired Texas Rangers living in an old, dusty south Texas town. Gus McCrae (played by Robert Duval) and Woodrow Call (Tommy Lee Jones) revive their spirit of adventure by taking on a cattle drive to Montana. Along the way, they face a variety of challenges, distractions, and perils. One of the first casualties on the trail is a young rider who ends up in a nest of water moccasins while driving the cattle across a small river.

Old Gus finds himself attempting to conduct some semblance of a funeral for the young rider. His eulogy is simple and to the point, "Life is short. Shorter for some than others. Let's go to Montana." As unsentimental as it sounds, Gus and Woodrow knew where they were headed, and they were not going to let sorrows or setbacks keep them from getting there. Montana was the end goal, the purpose of the drive, and the reason they were willing to face undue hardships. They were men on a mission.

What would you say is your mission in life? Where are you headed? It's easy to lose sight of the bigger picture of what you want in life, especially when you face disappointments, diversions and distractions along the way. Now and then, it is important to step back and look at the long view of your life and think about where you are headed. In this chapter, we want to help you stay focused on your life priorities, as well as your daily routines and habits.

Eleanor Roosevelt said, "The purpose of life, after all, is to live it, to taste experience to the utmost, to reach out eagerly and without fear for newer and richer experiences." Exploring your hopes, dreams, and priorities enables you to stretch yourself and encourages you to keep going when the chips seem down. When you consider your purpose in this world, you not only find direction, but you also discover how to use your time in wise and meaningful ways. The journey to accomplishing the most in your day actually begins by looking at the grander picture of your life mission or purpose.

When we (the authors) began discussing this chapter, Garry went over to his desk and pulled out a stack of 11" by 14" cards. Originally, these cards were shirt boards that came in Garry's folded and pressed shirts from the dry cleaners. Garry, being a good recycler, didn't want to see these cards go to waste, so he used them to write out his life mission statement and goals for each month. Yes, at the beginning of each month, he took a blank card and handwrote his mission statement at the top of the card, then listed his goals for the year, and what he wanted to accomplish in the next four weeks. He diligently carried out this practice for more than forty years. That's 480 shirt boards!

The reason he maintained this monthly habit was to help him stay centered on his life priorities, both personally and professionally. This intentional refocus enabled him to achieve his hopes and dreams for his life. Writing out a mission statement and goals, not just at the beginning of the year, but every month too, increases your capacity to remember, visualize and internalize what is important to you. It helps you to keep on track for where you want to go, what you want to be, and how you want to get there.

Writing Your Own Mission Statement

How do you determine what your overall purpose in life is, and how do you put it into a concise statement? Let's briefly look at some key ingredients that should go into a Personal Mission Statement. Three informative questions we will consider are:

- How are you uniquely gifted?
- Who do you want to influence or impact with your giftedness?
- What do you want to do with these gifts?

Perhaps the ultimate question you must ask yourself is, "What am I put on this earth to do?" Before you jump into creating your own mission statement, we wanted to show you a few examples. Here's what Garry wrote at the top of those shirt-board cards every month:

> *To help literally hundreds of millions of people to better lives: more secure financially, more satisfying spiritually and more fulfilling emotionally!*

We can confidently say that Garry has fulfilled his personal mission statement and then some! A number of years ago, when Garry sent out his retirement announcement, he began to receive hundreds of emails and notes in gratitude for all he had done to invest in the lives of business associates and salespeople. It was clearly evident that he fulfilled his life mission statement. The following are a few quotes from the many notes he received:

> *Garry, It is hard to estimate how many people you have impacted over the years, but I know the ripple effects have reached and impacted countless individuals and families... You have impacted my sales and now management career in this great industry. You had a huge impact in my professional and personal life.*
>
> *- John*

> *Garry, Thank you for believing in me, and for seeing more in me than I saw in myself. There is no way to measure the magnitude of the influence you've had over my life. You've challenged me to be better and do better both personally and professionally and for that I am eternally grateful.*
>
> *- Susan*

As you can see, Garry's mission statement compelled and propelled him to put into action the hopes and dreams he had for his life. Revisiting the statement every month helped him stay on track and live it out in a very practical sense. Of course, Garry's mission statement inspired Karol's. Below is what she handwrites at the first of every month as her personal mission:

> *To encourage men and women around the world to pursue their God-given passion and to use their gifts and talents in a positive and productive way.*

Notice that both statements are broad, rather than specific, leaving room for the variety of paths life may bring. For example, Karol started out as a math teacher but later became an author of over 35 positive and inspirational books. She currently offers daily encouragement to followers on social media from all over the world and most recently founded a parenting outreach helping men and women in impoverished communities. As you can see, her life mission has played out in a myriad of different avenues.

Here's a look at a few more mission statements of some notable companies and individuals.

Google – To organize the world's information and make it universally accessible and useful.

Make-A-Wish International – To grant the wishes of children with life-threatening medical conditions to enrich the human experience with hope, strength and joy.

Microsoft – To empower every person and every organization on the planet to achieve more.

Goodwill – To enhance the dignity and quality of life of individuals and families by strengthening communities, eliminating barriers to opportunity, and helping people in need reach their full potential through learning and the power of work.

Tesla – To accelerate the world's transition to sustainable energy.[16]

Did you notice that most of these statements included the answers to *How, Who* and *What*, just as our three earlier questions suggest? Now let's begin working on how you can formulate your own mission statement.

The How

It has been said that a personal mission statement is where your passions and your giftedness intersect. Let's begin by pondering what that means in your own life. Creating a personal mission statement requires thoughtful consideration, so you may want to grab some uninterrupted alone time as you set out to write yours. The first step is to analyze your "How." How do you see yourself using your gifts and talents to impact the world around you? Think about a verb that would best describe how you want to accomplish your hopes and dreams. Here are a few questions to ask yourself to get you started:

I feel like I am using my gifts when I am _____

_____.

_____.

I truly feel fulfilled when I _____

_____.

_____.

People often tell me that I am gifted at _____

_____.

_____.

I lose all sense of time when I am _____

_____.

_____.

Remember Garry's statement? His verb was "to help," because one of his natural gifts is helping others. Karol's, on the other hand, was "to encourage," since many people tell her that she is a great encourager and a positive motivator. Here's a list of a few verbs to consider:

- To give
- To build
- To teach
- To serve
- To strengthen
- To enhance
- To empower
- To grant
- To equip
- To inspire
- To grow
- To develop
- To initiate
- To activate
- To communicate
- To draw
- To lead
- To reinforce
- To affect
- To aspire
- To invent
- To start
- To create

Did any of these verbs resonate with you? Did one of them spark a sense of personal desire or reflect your strengths? Again, think about how you are uniquely wired. If you have a creative bent, then some of your obvious choices may be to design, to create, to invent, or to build. If you are a gifted teacher, then you may choose a verb such as: to teach, to communicate, to serve, to manage, to instruct.

Write your verb here: _____.

If you don't know which verb to choose, then circle several from the list that may apply to you personally. You can come back to it as you continue to create your Personal Mission Statement.

The Who

Now consider whom you want to impact. If you have the potential to reach people globally, then your *Who* may be "people all over the world." But if your main desire is to impact your customers in a positive way, then your own customers are your *Who*. Other examples of who may be:

- The people in my sphere of influence
- The customers in my territory
- The agents on my team
- My family, friends and co-workers

We encourage you to stretch yourself a little and dream big. When Garry started writing his mission statement on his cardboard shirt-liners, he was not yet reaching hundreds of millions of people. He wasn't even reaching hundreds of thousands at the time, but he had a goal in mind – a vision for what he could accomplish. He didn't just state what his present situation was; he stated what he hoped to accomplish in the future. And he kept his eyes on that goal! It was his Montana (as in Lonesome Dove), his desired destination. So think beyond your current center of influence. Think big; think bold.

Notice the *Who* of the mission statements we mentioned earlier:
- *the world's information*
- *children with life-threatening medical conditions*
- *every person and every organization on the planet*
  (wow, that's bold!)
- *individuals and families*
- *the world's ... energy*
- *women around the world*

Perhaps your *Who* could look like this:
- Every person I encounter
- People all over the world
- Millions of people

Write who you dream of impacting here: _____

_____

_____

The What

To complete your Life Mission Statement, you will need to consider your *What*. This should be a statement about what you envision yourself doing with your *How* and to your *Who*. It is not specifically about your current career or position. It's bigger and more far-reaching than the immediate activities in which you are involved. It's a broad brush stroke of the impact you hope to have in this world through what you do. Remember, Garry's, "To help literally hundreds of millions of people to better lives: more secure financially, more satisfying spiritually, and more fulfilling emotionally."

You may need to develop this over a period of time as you ponder your priorities and purpose. Remember, this statement is not set in stone; although one good question to ask yourself is "What would I want written on my tombstone?" Here are some other questions to help you narrow down your *What*:

- What do I hope to accomplish in life?
- For what do I want to be remembered?
- In what ways do I want to make a difference in the lives of others?
- In what way do I want to be an influence?
- At the end of my life, what accomplishment would make me feel satisfied?
- In what ways am I equipped to bring value and worth into the lives of others?

Write down your *What* here: _____

_____

_____

Now put your *How, Who,* and *What* all together and write your own mission statement below:

My personal mission statement is:

To _____

_____

_____

Once you have your statement, start the habit of writing it out every month. In fact, make a note on your calendar for the first day of every month to write and revisit your mission and goals. This will help you maintain focus and direction and keep your eyes on what is essential. It will help you to stay on course rather than be diverted by distractions or discouraged by disappointments. It will also assist you in making decisions when enticing opportunities come your way that don't exactly fit with your path or plan.

Setting and Sustaining Yearly Goals

Born in 1846 in Henderson, New York, Daniel Hudson Burnham was an American architect and urban designer. As the Director of Works for the World's Columbian Exposition in Chicago, Burnham served as one of the leaders in creating master plans for the development of significant cities such as Chicago, Manila, Baguio and downtown Washington, DC. He said, "Make no little plans; they have no magic to stir men's blood and probably will not be realized. Make big plans. Aim high in hope and work, remembering that a noble, logical diagram once recorded will never die. Long after you are gone, it will be a living thing asserting itself with ever-growing insistency."

Certainly, Daniel Burnham was a man who knew his purpose and made plans accordingly. He also knew the importance of writing down his plans. The Kinder brothers have always believed in the importance of not only writing down your goals at the beginning of each year but also revisiting them on a regular basis. In fact, it has become such a lasting habit, that even their children and grandchildren practice this same principle of goal-setting. Creating a plan for the year is an opportunity to dream, hope, and stretch to become a better person. As we make our plans in the form of goals, it is important to write them down and review them monthly.

Our goals should be conceivable, believable, and achievable. They also must be measurable, so we know if we have hit them or not. Some people use the acronym SMART when setting their goals. SMART stands for: specific, measurable, attainable, relevant/realistic, time-based. It's important to think about goals in every aspect of life, not just in business. Once you set a goal, break it down into doable habits. Generally speaking, it is wise to set goals in the following areas:

Mental – How do you want to grow in knowledge and skills? What books do you want to read or what courses do you need to take? Feed the mind as you feed the body. Determine how you want to grow mentally this year and what it will take to get there. Make it measurable. Here's an example of a mental yearly goal along with a doable habit.

I will read or listen to twelve books this year, one per month.

My reading time will be _____ each day.

Physical – What do you need to be doing to maintain your health? Are you eating right and exercising regularly? What is your ideal weight and what do you need to do to sustain it? When you take care of your health, you are better able to deal with the stresses and challenges of life and business. An example of a measurable physical goal along with a doable habit may be:

Maintain a weight of ____ _____ lbs (weighing myself weekly).

Exercise forty minutes, five times a week. Take a daily regimen of vitamins.

Business – What do you want to achieve financially this year? What potential do you have for the growth of your business? What sales numbers do you want to achieve? Ask yourself, "In the next 12 months how much will my net worth increase?" An example of a measurable business goal and habit would be:

I will achieve a _____ amount of sales and have a _____ increase in net worth this year.

I will review my goals at the end of the every _____ _____ (week, month, quarter)

Social – With whom do you want to surround yourself this year? Is there a mentor you want to pursue, or is there someone you need to be mentoring? How often do you want to get together with others socially? You tend to become like the people with whom you spend time. When you surround yourself with people who are successful, you tend to be inspired to be successful. At the same time, it is good to have several people who look up to you and whom you are able to inspire and help both in business and in life. Are there some new friends you want to make in the coming year? New people continually come into your life while others tend to roll out or grow distant. You can't keep up with everyone. You may have a few long-term friends and some who come in and out of your life. An example of a possible social goal is:

I will connect or contact at least one person per _____ _____ (week, month, quarter) who inspires me and also one whom I can inspire.

I will make it a habit to text a note of encouragement to one person every day.

Family-time – How can you invest in your family each day? What do you want weekends to look like for your family? Perhaps a measurable goal could be:

I will have dinner _____ times per week together with my family.

(Depending on your stage of life) I will read to my kids _____ per week.

Spiritual – Are you growing spiritually? What does that look like on a personal level? Each of us has a need to connect with our Creator, and this should be the center of our life. We need time to be quiet and pray or meditate each day. This helps us keep a healthy balance in all areas of life. When Garry lived in Akron, Ohio, he was in charge of a large agency. In addition, he met with friends who were not in the business but who held a Wednesday morning Bible study. They met faithfully each week at the local fitness center. This was a way to not only grow spiritually, but also to experience fellowship with others who believed the same way he did. Here's a possible example of a spiritual goal.

I will pray or meditate every morning.

I will do one activity to assist my spiritual growth each week.

Goals help you continually stretch and improve in every area of your life – mentally, physically, socially and spiritually. As far as your career, your goals for your sales numbers and your net worth should increase each year. The Kinder Brothers often say, "Every day, in every way, I'm getting better and better." This is a powerful statement to tell yourself every single morning.

Monthly Motivational Meeting

As we mentioned earlier, on the first day of every month, make an appointment for a monthly motivational meeting with yourself. This is a time to revisit and rewrite your yearly goals and life mission statement. It gives you an opportunity to regularly look at how you are doing and what you need to adjust. As you begin a new month, take a moment to examine how you did last month, and consider what you need to achieve in the coming month in order to stay on track for the year. How can you increase your production and net worth? What are some action points that you need to add to your agenda for the month?

Let's break this down into doable steps as you have your monthly review meeting. First, thoughtfully write out your personal mission statement. Then, in short form revisit each of your yearly goals, writing a brief statement of what you are trying to accomplish. You can choose to handwrite them or type them up, but we recommend handwriting because it helps you personalize and remember them. Keep in mind, this is a time to check up on yourself to see if you are staying on course. Below is an example of a brief checklist for your goals:

1. Mental – One book a month – write the title _____
_____

2. Physical – healthy, weight of _____

3. Business – sales _____, net worth _____

4. Family – dinner time together _____ nights a week

5. Social – people to contact _____
_____
_____
_____

6. Spiritual – reading and meditating _____ per day

At the end of this chapter, you will find a sample template that you can copy for each month to help you revisit your goals. Take some time to think about any goals that need to be readjusted. For example, perhaps you have far exceeded your expectations for the year, and you need to set bigger goals. Your monthly appointment with yourself will allow you the opportunity to adjust your old goals and to create new goals for yourself to continue to stretch you and push you further.

If you find yourself falling far behind on your yearly goals, first you need to consider if your original goals were realistic. Sometimes, we overestimate what we can achieve, so we may need to make some minor adjustments. Rarely, if ever, do you want to decrease your goals, but it is a good idea to think about the reasons why you are not reaching your goals. Do you need to re-examine how you use your time? Are you being distracted by things that keep you from hitting your goals? Did you have some unforeseeable life circumstances that got in the way?

If you are part of a sales team, set a regular appointment with your manager and visit with him or her about your goals on a monthly basis. This provides accountability as well as someone to help you consider realistic goals and discuss both your weak spots and strengths. If you are a manager, plan monthly meetings with individual members of your sales team in order to review their progress.

There are a few other areas we want to encourage you to think about as you have your monthly motivational meeting with yourself. Consider who you want to be and where you want to be in the next five to ten years. Write this down at the bottom of your monthly page. You may want to add at least one motivational statement for the month. Garry wrote down all the companies and people he planned to engage with throughout the month, as a reminder to contact them and schedule or reconfirm the meeting with them.

Your Week at a Glance

We are not created to work, work, work, 24/7. We all need to take time to rest and rejuvenate, but often that just doesn't happen. We must be deliberate about taking a sabbath (Hebrew word for rest), or it simply won't happen. It is a healthy habit to choose one day a week as your day of rest and reflection. Most people choose either Saturday or Sunday as a day to regroup and rejuvenate. It helps you prepare for a fresh start in the coming week and gives you an opportunity to make a plan for the days ahead of you.

Look over your appointment and meetings for the coming week. It is a good practice to review what is unfinished from the previous week and, if need be, set it into the schedule for the coming week. Are there any appointments for which you need to prepare? Be sure to enter the preparation time on your calendar as well. Who are the people you need to contact or follow up with for the next week? It is important to be ready for the coming week, so you know exactly what you are doing when your feet hit the floor on Monday morning.

As you prepare for the week ahead of you, set three objectives for the week. These should be three things you need to accomplish during the week, such as a short-term project or preparing for a meeting or making a certain number of phone calls. These weekly objectives will keep you on target and help you push forward, instead of allowing time-wasters to get in your way. By only setting three objectives, you will hopefully be able to check each one off and, by the end of the week, feel a sense of satisfaction and accomplishment.

You may also want to designate certain days for important weekly tasks that need to get done. For example, you could label Fridays as "Financial Fridays," designating it as the day to handle financial details in your business (paying bills, dealing with reimbursements, or making a deposit). By designating a certain day to face your finances, you know you will get the job done. Perhaps you need to designate a day to write thank you notes to clients with whom you recently met, so you could create "Thank-you Note Thursdays" to devote a short period of time to writing those notes.

Seize Each Day

Do you feel frustrated with your daily To Do list? If you are like most people, you rarely come close to getting it all done. In fact, one study shows the average percent of uncompleted items on a daily list is around 41%. So how do you successfully seize the day and conquer the inevitable distractions? Let's look at three ideas to help you win the day and be more productive.

Plan the Day Before – At the end of each workday, take a moment to look at your calendar and create a schedule for the next day. Set out blocks of time for your meetings as well as your tasks that need to be accomplished. Draw one square in which to write the names of all the people you need to contact either by email, text, social media, or phone call. As for places you will need to go, consider the approximate time you will need to leave in order to get there on time, and take a moment to set the alarm on your phone for those times. Also, set out the clothes you want to wear. When you plan the day before, you will sleep better and wake up the next morning ready to go to work. Or as the Kinder Brothers put it, "You will wake up employed."

Circle Three Priorities – As you look at your schedule, circle three tasks or activities that are top priorities. You may want to circle them with a bright yellow highlighter, so they stand out. Your top priorities should include those things that must be done before the day passes or meetings that are essential to your work. Take another pen and underline the items on your list that are important and need attention; but if push came to shove, they could be finished the next day. As you highlight your priorities, you can keep a steady focus on them throughout your day to ensure that you move toward completing them. You will feel a tremendous sense of accomplishment when you see that your priorities have been achieved each day.

Create Blocks of Time – Generally speaking, when you have a set amount of time to get a task accomplished, you tend to narrow your focus, ignore distractions and get the job done. Consider the concept of the "power of a half-hour." When you designate 30 minutes to a task, and keep your focus on what needs to get done, you are much more likely to get it completed. Set a timer to help you stay on track. Blocking off short parcels of time helps you set aside emails, social media and phone calls and other interruptions in order to finish. If you need a little more time, then certainly you can add to it, but you will be surprised how much can be done when you concentrate for a half hour. Between each 30-minute segment, take a break or breather. Of course, stay flexible and leave a cushion between each time-block to deal with unexpected tasks that may arise.

Live It Out

Never underestimate the importance of regularly reviewing and rewriting your life mission and your goals. This is the secret to your success in staying on course with what you want to accomplish. It will also help you set up your daily priorities. Review is important, but actions are crucial.

Popular blogger and author Leo Babauta put it this way, "It's one thing to set priorities, it's another to live them. What you actually do, how you live your life, reveals your actual priorities. Your priorities are what you live, not what you put on paper."[17]

Perhaps you have observed that the Kinder Brothers have a great admiration for Winston Churchill, as we have shared his stories and quotes throughout this book, yet we thought it was fitting to add one of his most powerful quotes at the end of this chapter. In his first speech as Prime Minster of Great Britain, Churchill addressed the House with a brief and direct speech to make his policy abundantly clear as they faced the looming Nazi domination. The following is a portion of his speech:

> *I would say to the House as I have said to those who have joined this government, that I have nothing to offer but blood, toil, tears and sweat. WE have before us an ordeal of the most grievous kind. You ask, what is our policy? I will say – it is to wage war, by sea, land and air, with all the might and strength that God can give us – to wage war against a monstrous tyranny, never surpassed in the dark lamentable catalogue of human crime. That is our policy!... You ask, what is our aim? I can answer in one word – victory. Victory at all costs, victory in spite of all terror, victory, however long or hard the road may be, for without victory there is no survival.*

Victory doesn't come easy. Neither does living out our life mission. It takes blood, sweat, toil, and tears. Churchill had his goal in sight. He knew what was best for the country, and he was willing to do what it took to achieve victory. What are you willing to do to be the best you can be? What will it take to reach your goals? The answer is different for each of us; but one thing is certain, we must know where we are going. We must live with purpose, passion, and positivity.

Recapping the Essentials

Positive Truth:
Determine your priorities in life and allow them to shape your goals each year. Review and revisit them regularly.

Discussion Questions:
- Why is it important to set goals in every area of your life, not just business?

\
\
\

- What are some reasons people do not typically reach their yearly goals?

\
\
\

- Share your Life Mission Statement with your group.

Positive Actions:

Mark your calendar for the first working day of every month. This is your day to revisit and rewrite your goals. On the following pages you will find templates to use for staying on track both monthly and daily.

──── Monthly Template ────

Fill this out on the first day of each month.

Life Mission Statement: _____

_____

_____

Yearly Goals

               Recap   On Track?

Mental: _____

Physical: _____

Spiritual: _____

Business: _____

Social: _____

Family: _____

Three Objectives for the Month:

1. _____

2. _____

3. _____

Monthly Motivational Quote:

People or businesses I plan to meet with:

──────────── Daily Plan ────────────

Here's a sample of the Daily Plan to be filled out at the end of each workday to help you be prepared for the next day.

Date:_____

Three Priorities for the day:

1. _____

   _____

2. _____

   _____

3. _____

   _____

Email:_____

Call: _____

Text: _____

Clean: _____

Read: _____

General Schedule:

Final Note From Karol

I hope that the concepts in this book will be a catalyst to success in both your career and your personal life. Always remember to keep a balance in life. Victory in your work at the expense of your family or relationships is not victory at all. True victory in life is when we live for something bigger than ourselves and put others needs before our own. May you use these principles to deepen your connections and live a positive and productive life.

Allow me to share one final (and personal) story with you as we close this book. After completing the majority of this book, my dad (co-author Garry Kinder) entered his twilight years. Dementia began to ravage his once dynamic and inspiring mind, yet he remained kind and uplifting to everyone around him. As his memory faded, I decided to print a simple hard-covered copy of this book in order to read it to him while he was still with us.

My expectations were limited as his communication had diminished, and he didn't seem to remember writing *Positive Connectivity*. I will never forget the day I walked into his room and proudly displayed the book to him. Much to my surprise, he took the book in his hands and smoothed his fingers over the cover as if it were a treasure.

He held his copy of the book and perused through the pages as I began reading from my copy. I was well into chapter two when Dad took his copy, closed it deliberately with a pop, and proclaimed just one word. "Perfect!"

It's hard to describe what I felt at that moment. His one word spoke volumes! It meant he did remember it and that he was proud of it! He was pleased, and I was thrilled! After that day, each time I entered his room, he looked at me and then looked at his copy of *Positive Connectivity* on the shelf. I knew he wanted me to continue reading it to him. He is in heaven now, but I thank God that He allowed me to have this special project with my dad before he headed homeward.

It is my hope that you will find this book as satisfying and encouraging as we both did in the writing of it. Thank you for taking the time to read it and share it. And as Dad always said, "Keep up the great work!"

Stay Connected

You can stay connected with the Kinder Brothers International in the following ways:

Website: www.KinderBrothers.com

Facebook: www.facebook.com/KinderBrothersInternational

Linkedin: www.linkedin.com/company/kinder-brothers-international

Download their app to your smart phone:
Kinder Brothers International

You can also connect with Karol through:

Website: www.PositiveLifePrinciples.com

Facebook: www.facebook.com/KarolLaddAuthor

Linkedin: www.linkedin.com/in/karolladd

Instagram: @KarolLadd

For more about her parenting outreach go to:
www.EngageParenting.com

About the Author

Garry Kinder

GARRY KINDER, is the former CEO of Kinder Brothers International and was a well-known sales and management consultant to more than 300 companies worldwide. He is the author of eleven books including the New York Times Bestseller, *Winning Strategies in Selling* (year 1983) which he wrote with his brother Jack and former Dallas Cowboys quarterback Roger Staubach.

Garry began his career as an insurance agent while he was at Illinois Wesleyan University. and became one of the youngest agents in Illinois to achieve membership in the Million Dollar Round Table. He eventually rose to regional vice president of Equitable Life before starting Kinder Brothers International. Garry has been active in civic affairs and is a Trustee Emeritus at Illinois Wesleyan University.

He is a past president of the FCA of Texas, and Kidney Foundation of Texas, and helped start the Baseball Chapel for major league baseball. He served as Chairman of the Board of the Bill Glass Evangelistic Association for 20 years. The Kinder Brothers Monday Morning Message is read by over 7,000 people around the world.

About the Author

Karol Ladd

Known as the "Positive Lady," **KAROL LADD** is the best-selling author of over 35 books including *The Power of a Positive Woman* and *Thrive, Don't Simply Survive*. Her company, Positive Life Principles, offers positive strategies for success for men and women all over the world.

Karol is the founder and director of Engage Positive Parenting Initiative, an outreach providing discussion-based parenting classes for men and women as they raise and impact the next generation. Karol is active in her community, serves on several boards and leads an inspirational Bible study called "House to House."

She is the recipient of numerous awards including Rising Star Award from Women's Non-profit Alliance, Platinum Award from CWIMA Media group, Serving Hope Corporate Award from Emily's Place and Silver Angel Award for several of her books. Karol's most valued role is that of wife to Curt and mother to grown daughters, Grace and Joy and most recently embracing the role of "Kay Kay" to her six precious grandchildren.

[1] Albert Mehrabian, *Silent Messages*, (Belmont, CA: Wadsworth Publishing, 1971)

[2] www.ScienceofPeople.com

[3] www.americanetiquette.com/global-etiquette

[4] Garry Kinder, 50 Lessons in 50 Years, (Dallas, Texas: Cornerstone Leadership Institute, 2006), 67.

[5] Greg McKeown, *Essentialism* (New York, NY: Crown Business, 2014), p. 48.

[6] www.news.harvard.edu/gazette/story/2010/11/wandering-mind-not-a-happy-mind

[7] www.fastcompany.com/3036748/why-its-so-hard-to-detect-emotion-in-emails-and-texts

[8] www.sciencedirect.com/science/article/pii/S074756321000213X

[9] Dr. Emma Seppala, The Happiness Track (San Francisco: Harper One, 2016)

[10] www.telegraph.co.uk/news/winston-churchill/11366880/Winston-Churchills-10-most-important-speeches.html

[11] Frank Bettger, *How I Raised Myself from Failure to Success in Selling* (Englewood Cliffs, NJ: Prentice Hall, 1961)

[12] Eric Barker, *Barking Up the Wrong Tree* (New York, NY: Harper One, 2017), p. 68.

[13] www.jonathanmilligan.com/how-to-develop-your-very-own-code-of-persistence

[14] James Clear, *Atomic Habits* (New York, NY: Penguin/Random House, 2018), p. 21.

[15] www.muscleprodigy.com/michael-phelps-workout-and-diet

[16] As of May 2023 the mission statements of the following companies can be found at:
Google – www.google.com/search/howsearchworks/our-approach
Make-A-Wish – www.bartleby.com/essay/Make-A-Wish-Mission-Statement
Microsoft – www.microsoft.com/en-us/diversity
Goodwill – www.mission-statement.com/goodwill
Tesla – www.tesla.com/impact

[17] www.success.com/setting-priorities

Made in the USA
Middletown, DE
18 August 2023

36609470R00070